RIVER COTTAGE

GREAT
SALADS

RIVER COTTAGE
GREAT
SALADS

GELF ALDERSON

Hugh Fearnley-Whittingstall's
RIVER COTTAGE

BLOOMSBURY PUBLISHING
LONDON · OXFORD · NEW YORK · NEW DELHI · SYDNEY

Recipe notes

- All spoon measures are level unless otherwise stated: 1 tsp = 5ml spoon; 1 tbsp = 15ml spoon.
- All herbs are fresh unless otherwise suggested.
- Use freshly ground or cracked black pepper unless otherwise listed.
- All veg and fruit should be washed. Choose organic fruit and veg if possible.
- Root veg, onions, garlic and ginger are peeled or scrubbed unless otherwise suggested.
- If using the zest of citrus fruit, choose unwaxed fruit.
- Please use free-range eggs, preferably organic.
- Oven timings are provided for both conventional and fan-assisted ovens. Individual ovens can deviate by 10°C or more either way from the actual setting, so get to know your oven and use an oven thermometer to check the temperature.

Contents

Foreword

The best salads, I think, are glorious assemblies of colour, flavour and texture, mostly based on plants. As long as these elements are covered you can go in any direction you like. Pick ingredients that are raw or cooked, fresh or preserved, crisp, tender, tangy or sweet. Serve them grated, slivered, chopped or torn, lightly seasoned or lavishly dressed – there is no limit.

The brilliant, generous, salady spectrum is encapsulated so perfectly in this book that – without wanting to stretch a metaphor – it's almost like a fabulous salad in itself. Just flick through the pages and the sheer gorgeousness of the produce Gelf chooses to work with is a feast for your eyes before you even get to the words. A quick read will have your mouth watering and your stomach rumbling, and a deeper delve will see you raiding your cupboard, your fridge, your garden or your local shop – no matter the time of year. Salads are not just for summer and these pages will bring inspiration to the darkest winter days, as well as to the warmer months.

Gelf Alderson has worked alongside me at River Cottage since 2012. He is the captain of a kitchen that works tirelessly to rethink and reinterpret the food we eat, and to delight us all with the results. He can turn out a splendid roast dinner or a tiered celebration cake without batting an eyelid. But one of the things I appreciate most about him is his extraordinary creativity with seasonal fruit, vegetables and herbs. He really does embody what River Cottage is all about. He never rests on his laurels, he is always nudging at the boundaries, questioning the foods we might use and where they come from, and exploring new flavour pairings – and his innovative instincts are invariably spot on. Yet he keeps it all within the sphere of real food eaten by real people, devising dishes that are hearty, unfussy, mostly simple, yes; but still original and enticing. That is reflected in these pages, in which Gelf has pulled off something very special: a cookbook that uses familiar produce and ingredients, but often shows them in a new and exciting light.

Gelf's recipes also banish any idea that eating a salad is something we might do just because it is 'good for us'. Undoubtedly, these dishes are very good for you, bursting with a huge variety of unprocessed whole foods. Gelf celebrates the many different seasonal vegetables and fruit, along with nuts, seeds, healthy oils and good proteins, that our bodies need to thrive. But you'll be preparing and eating them first and foremost because you can see they are going to be good for your taste buds. I've particularly enjoyed his zesty and unexpected combinations such as Celeriac, rhubarb, hazelnuts and parsley (page 49), and Seedy kale and kimchi with orange and seaweed dressing (page 56). And this playfulness with punchy flavours is no less in evidence with heartier combinations like Swede, sprouts, chestnuts and char-grilled clementines (page 78) or Merguez roast squash, pears and chicory (page 138).

These dishes promise a real adventure for our palates. And the knowledge that they include such excellent, health-supporting ingredients further enhances that sense of anticipation. These are recipes that will nourish you – mind, body and soul. So take up your knife, grab your grater, and indeed fire up the barbecue when the weather is right. Prepare to be seriously impressed by the delicious things that await. Thank you Gelf, for a gorgeous collection of truly great salads.

Hugh

Introduction

Salads, for me, are the ultimate expression of seasonality. There are celebratory assemblies for every season – from light springy affairs, showcasing the first nutty spears of asparagus or fresh garden peas teased from their pods – to the riotous rainbow of summer abundance, rich with aubergine purples, cherry tomatoes and fragrant herbs. The autumn brings sweet, beta-carotene potent squash, which are great for protecting you during the looming cold season, and encouraging you to roast and grill veg to add warmth and depth to your salads. Then comes winter where root veg, dark leafy greens and bitter chicories play a starring role.

Vibrant, veg-focussed, and bounding with colour, texture and flavour, salads bring freshness and zing to the table. At River Cottage, a seasonal salad is always part of any meal, be it a light lunch in the garden for staff or one of our lavish seven-course feasts. This book is brimming with inspiration gleaned from years of glorious River Cottage creations.

The recipes are quick and full of ingredients you can grow yourself, even if you don't have a garden. There is an in-depth guide to growing your own salad ingredients, too, as well as suggestions on using herbs, edible flowers and foraged finds to make spectacular salads that dazzle the palate. I'll show you how to lift ingredients – including veg from the garden that are often overlooked for salads – to create truly knockout assemblies. Putting to use an array of techniques, veg are taken to the next level – by charring on the barbecue, roasting to get that perfect crispy texture, or shaving raw veg that are typically eaten cooked, for example.

As well as culinary joy, you can derive incredible nutritional benefits from your salads. Leafy greens and raw veggies are superb sources of fibre, which helps feed the good bacteria in your gut. They're also rich in vitamins, minerals and health-beneficial antioxidants. Many of the salads in the book contain seeds or nuts, and/or a healthy selection of oils in their dressing, which assist the body to absorb vitamins. And salads that marry fresh citrus with leafy greens offer an iron boost because the vitamin C from the citrus boosts your body's iron absorption.

I've structured the recipes into seven chapters, each bursting with exciting flavours and original combinations of ingredients. I start with 'Quick' to illustrate the speed with which you can spin a stunning salad with minimal effort. The trick is bringing together fantastic ingredients that marry so beautifully they need no further embellishment: juicy summer tomatoes, fresh mint and sun-kissed raspberries (see page 51), for example; or earthy celeriac paired with the sharp tang of rhubarb, toasted hazelnuts and fresh parsley (see page 49). I've also tucked in a breakfast salad of autumn fruits with toasted oats on page 58, which works as a dessert, too.

'Hearty' salads is full of warming ingredients and big, bold flavours. These are salads with several components that can happily stand on their own, such as Char-grilled cabbage, pickled pears, pesto and walnuts (page 83). By contrast, the 'Light' chapter features salads that can either be served as sides or mixed and matched to create a salady tapas of sorts. These are interesting assemblies, comprising minimal ingredients and elegant dressings; Fennel, celery and apple with creamy almond dressing (page 114) is one of my favourites. I find the magic of spice is so transformative that I've devoted a whole chapter to 'Spicy' salads. Do try Beetroot, sea bass, blackberries and chilli (page 153); it's so simple and elegant, yet rich with a tantalising depth.

The 'Lunchbox' chapter that follows features recipes that are easy to take to work or assemble quickly at home, with ingredients that will help to sustain your energy through the day. I then dive into a bit of playful fun with 'River Cottage classics' – our take on some long-established salads like salade niçoise (see page 203), and Panzanella (page 193). The book's final stop is 'Dressings, pickles and krauts'. A well-made dressing is the binding backbone of any good salad. Here you'll find recipes for the classics, plus a selection of zesty dressings, including Orange, kimchi and seaweed dressing (page 226), which is a true River Cottage original.

Hugh's first River Cottage book introduced the idea of a 'food continuum', to describe our relationship to the food we eat. From the start, his mission has been to help connect people more closely with the source of their food. Through growing your own ingredients, foraging, making things from scratch, you not only tap into your intuitive hunter-gather instincts but you also enjoy more delicious, nutritious food. Something as trifling as making a salad from scratch – especially if it features some homegrown ingredients – chips away at the dominance of industrialised food and shifts things in a positive direction.

What's brilliant about salads is that veg takes centre stage, even if meat or fish is featured. And throughout the book I've offered guidance on sustainable sourcing and ingredient swaps. I've also featured an array of pulses and legumes. These are a phenomenal source of plant-based protein, carry flavours beautifully and are also amazing for soil health with their complex root systems that fix nitrogen into the soil and help other plants grow.

Salads have the perfect balance of ingredients – for our own health and that of our environment. But even I, admittedly, once viewed them with a little scepticism. That is even though I was raised as a vegetarian in a household where you'd never find a bottle of salad cream. My name might give some clue to my unconventional upbringing (at least by 1980s standards). One of my elder sisters was told I was an elf. She couldn't say 'elf' and her mispronunciation led to my name, Gelf!

Despite my dad's prolific homegrown produce and my mum's magical way of preparing it, I fell into the trap of dismissing salads as 'rabbit food', only to be suffered if you were on a diet. My time as a chef has certainly helped change that and appreciate what a true salad represents: a soulful dish that showcases produce and ingredients like no other.

I hope this book inspires you into the habit of relishing at least one plateful of salad a day. Or even to go further and see if you can include a simple salad with every meal. Be playful and venture beyond the pages of this book with the information it arms you with – testing new techniques and dabbling with new-found growing adventures, even if limited to your kitchen table.

A salad a day is definitely a great way to keep the doctor away, but equally importantly, food has the magic to connect us with our environment and each other deeply, and this is the richer aim of this book beyond simple pleasure and nourishment.

Salad for all seasons

Tailoring your salad repertoire to the seasons is not only the most delicious way to eat, it is also healthier. The seasons give us the nutrients we need: carrots and squash offer immune-boosting beta-carotene in the autumn ahead of the cold and flu season, for example, while spring offers new growth of health-beneficial greens after a winter of heavier, more indulgent foods.

Eating with the seasons is also, typically, more affordable – especially if you embrace gluts and preserve ingredients for future salad-making. I've peppered seasonal swaps throughout the recipes to give you options through the year. Here is a guide to embracing the best each season has to offer, with suggestions for suitable alternatives when the seasonal opportunity fades.

SPRING

Asparagus
Try purple as well as green varieties. Use raw asparagus shaved into ribbons, or roasted spears, or dip tender, raw spears into my creamy almond dressing (see page 114). Suitable swaps: spring onions, baby leeks, purple sprouting broccoli or salsify.

Broccoli, purple-sprouting
You can also get sprouting cauliflower, which has a brilliant nutty flavour. Suitable swaps: Tenderstem broccoli, florets of broccoli, spring onions, baby leeks, salsify or asparagus.

Cabbages
Hispi is a River Cottage favourite. Harvested from late spring, this pointed cabbage has looser leaves and a sweeter flavour than firm winter varieties like January King. It is brilliant barbecued, as well as shredded and tossed into a salad raw. Suitable swaps: summer lettuces or autumn/winter cabbage varieties.

Carrots, bunched
These come in a variety of colours, such as Purple Haze or the smaller Red-Cored Chantenay variety. Note that the leaves from bunched carrots can be chopped and used in place of basil in salads. Suitable swaps: mature carrots (without tops) and other roots such as parsnip or beetroot.

Radishes
If you're keen to grow salad ingredients in a small space, radishes can be raised from seed in just 6 weeks and there are so many different colours and shapes to explore. You can also use the leaves in a mix with other salad greens. Suitable swaps: turnips or kohlrabi.

Rhubarb
Try forced 'Champagne' and other indoor winter rhubarb in early spring before the outdoor season. Suitable swaps: gooseberries for their sharp, tangy flavour in summer, or tart, green dessert apples in autumn.

Seaweed
Spring is peak foraging season for seaweed, if you can gather it yourself or source it from a market. Swap out dried seaweed in recipes with fresh whenever you can. You can also dry fresh seaweed and store it to give you an all-year-round supply.

SUMMER

Apricots

Seek ripe, fragrant apricots during their short season from late July to August. Suitable swaps: peaches or nectarines in summer; plums, damsons or greengages in early autumn; or citrus fruits in the winter.

Aubergines

Char-grilled slices of aubergine make a brilliant addition to salads. Or you can make a delicious baba ganoush (a smoky aubergine dip). Simply scoop out the flesh from a charred aubergine and swap it for the fava beans in the hummus recipe on page 200. Serve with Little Gem lettuce or other robust salad leaves to scoop up the dip. Suitable swaps: courgettes during the summer and early autumn, or parsnips in the winter.

Blackberries

A late summer joy, foraged blackberries gathered from hedgerows in the late afternoon or early evening sun are always best. Freeze any gluts; they work well in salads once defrosted. Suitable swaps: diced apple, or sliced rhubarb.

Blueberries

We have a small blueberry shrub on the edge of the River Cottage kitchen garden. The berries are rich in health-beneficial antioxidants. They add a little pop of colour and a refreshing contrast of fresh, subtle sweetness to summer leaves. Paired with cucumber, goat's cheese and dill they make a lovely simple salad. Suitable swaps: grapes or white currants.

Broad beans

These delicious summer beans are brilliant in salads – raw if they are young and tender, or steamed. Pair with summer herbs, potatoes and a French vinaigrette for an easy summer salad. Suitable swaps: tinned butter beans or defrosted frozen peas.

Cherries

Tart foraged cherries make a lovely summery addition to Barley tabbouleh (page 187) or Spicy, nutty quinoa (page 141). Plumper, sweeter cherries from the market or local greengrocer's make a delicious fruity addition to Panzanella (page 193). Suitable swaps: damsons or plums.

Courgettes

This is another veg rich with variety. We grow delicious golden courgettes at River Cottage, but there are also attractive striped and round varieties. Baby courgettes are the best of all, as they are the sweetest and lovely eaten raw. Suitable swap: marrow.

Cucumbers

You can source an increasing number of different cucumbers these days. Seek out unusual varieties, like the round Crystal Lemon cucumber or the tiny, grape-sized cucamelon, which look like fairy-sized watermelons. Suitable swaps: courgettes or green tomatoes.

Currants

This summer fruit adds little jewels of colour to salads, along with a burst of sharp tanginess. Ripe, juicy blackcurrants are a lovely addition to Smoked mackerel niçoise (page 203). Suitable swap: sour cherries.

French beans

Typically, these are referred to simply as 'green beans'. We grow a purple variety at River Cottage and you can also get yellow French beans, which tend to be more tender and less stringy. Tossed in a simple vinaigrette with some garden herbs and toasted walnuts, they make an instant salad in their own right, but they're also a staple in a summery niçoise (see page 203). Suitable swaps: purple sprouting or Tenderstem broccoli, or asparagus.

Gooseberries

These tart, refreshing, berries sit somewhere between cucumber and grapes flavourwise, and you can easily juggle them between sweet and savoury. In that respect, they're the perfect fruit for a salad and they pair nicely with many herbs. Sweeter red gooseberries, available later in the summer, are particularly good. We often make dill pickles with gooseberries on River Cottage preserving days – these are a treat in a Little Gem salad and a welcome addition to a classic Greek salad. Suitable swaps: cucamelons, diced cucumber or grapes.

Peas

You can't beat the sweetness of freshly picked and podded garden peas. Raw, crunchy and full of explosive flavour, they're an enormous bonus added to any salad. When they are in season, add a handful of young, tender peas to Bacon, new potatoes and lettuce with chunky tartare dressing (page 178), or Courgettes, toasted buckwheat, goat's cheese and dill (page 116). Suitable swaps: broad beans, pea shoots or defrosted frozen peas.

Raspberries

Adding raspberries to any salad will provide a sharp, sweet, surprising contrast. I love the juxtaposition of raspberries and tomatoes (see page 51), but they're good with leftover roast pork, too - try them in the Honey-glazed leftover belly pork with shredded summer veg (page 180). They're also great with punchy Asian flavours and work well with the Soy, lime, chilli, ginger and garlic dressing (page 225). Suitable swaps: redcurrants or blackberries.

Strawberries

Ripe, red and juicy strawberries are, of course, delicious in their own right and they make a stunning addition to so many salads – they're like little sweet tomatoes. Slightly underripe, green strawberries are also a treat, lending a sharp, tangy contrast. Try adding a handful to Mussels, fennel, chilli and cucumber (page 150), or to replace the green grapes in Peas, mint, Oakleaf lettuce and grapes (page 108). Suitable swaps: raspberries, grapes, or diced apples or pears.

Tomatoes

A salad staple and with good reason, tomatoes provide acidity, sweetness, texture and juiciness. Ripe tomatoes at their peak can hold their own with very little intervention – tossed with a pinch of sea salt they practically make their own dressing – and it's difficult to beat a simple tomato salad made with ripe, flavourful tomatoes. Each different type of tomato has its own personality, so seek out as many varieties as you can and see how they subtly change a recipe. Varieties we grow and love include Brandywine, Black Russian, Oxheart, Gardener's Delight, Sweet Grape and Black Cherry. Suitable swap: plums.

AUTUMN

Apples

The most reliable of the UK staple fruits – with so much variety, but also durability. The apple season starts in August and harvesting rolls on until Christmas, but there is such a hearty array of storers that we can have all manner of different local apples squirrelled away right through to Easter. Work your way through the diversity, trying all that the apple world has to offer within this book's recipes and beyond. One of the humblest salads you can make is a simple pairing of grated or finely diced apple with peppery leaves like watercress or rocket – a spritz of lemon juice and a scattering of toasted seeds or nuts will give you an elegant dish in an instant. Suitable swaps: apricots or peaches.

Beetroot

I have devoted a recipe to the wonderful varieties of beetroot that can be found (see page 93). Chioggia, the stripy one, has an intense sweetness; Golden Detroit beetroot is mellower; while the classic Rhonda or Gesche varieties of beetroot are rich and earthy. And don't overlook cylindrical beetroot, which is brilliant for shaving into short ribbons or wisps. Suitable swap: carrots.

Cabbages

These hearty brassicas are pretty much available all year round, in various guises. Hispi cabbages are around in the spring (see page 13) but late autumn and winter are when most cabbages mature (they take a full 9 months to grow). They lend themselves nicely to shredding for slaws, so that's my main area of focus, but a handful of shredded cabbage leaves adds a deliciously sweet, yet peppery, crunch to any salad. We grow some great varieties at River Cottage, including Copenhagen and Enkhuizen, which make the best sauerkraut; Greyhound and Filderkraut; and Red Cabbage Amarant. These are all worth seeking out. Suitable swaps: fennel or kale.

Cauliflower

Also in the brassica or cruciferous family, cauliflower offers a nutty, yet spicy, mustardy hint of warmth to salads. I love roasting cauliflower to soften it a little and develop a toasty, caramelised edge before tossing it through a dressing and then pepping it up with fresh herbs and seeds. Try Roast cauliflower with pumpkin seed satay (page 137). Suitable swaps: broccoli or any root vegetable.

Damsons

Smaller in size and richer in flavour than plums, damsons have a vibrant dark blue skin and a tart edge to the flavour (yet deeper, with red wine notes). They're a brilliant contrast to squash or peppery leaves like rocket. They also pickle nicely, and pair well in grain-based salads like Barley tabbouleh (page 187); use in place of the cherry tomatoes. Suitable swaps: cherry tomatoes or plums.

Fennel

Refreshing with an aromatic hit of anise, fennel can lighten and lift a salad. It works equally well with a simple lemony dressing or a more unctuous option, like the creamy almond dressing on page 114. A bulb that grows just above ground, fennel, surprisingly is a member of the carrot family. Similarly,

it also has feathery leaves that resemble dill, which are delicious chopped and added to salads. Suitable swaps: apple or cabbage.

Grapes

These juicy fruits are imported much of the year, but they can be grown here in the UK and autumn is peak season. We have some surprisingly sweet varieties growing at River Cottage, nestled along the garden walls, which protect them from frost. I love using them in salads as a sweeter, juicier swap for tomatoes. Suitable swaps: cherry tomatoes or plums.

Greengages

Ripe greengages are sweet and flavourful, while the underripe fruit is tart and tannic, like rhubarb or gooseberries. They are brilliant bedfellows with refreshing ingredients like cucumber and mint. Try them in place of gooseberries in Cucumber, grapes, apple and almonds (page 52), or as a sharp, contrasting addition to Barley, rocket pesto, Cheddar and chives (page 166). Suitable swaps: plums, gooseberries.

Kohlrabi

Flavourwise, kohlrabi is like a radishy apple. Related to both cabbage and radishes, it is sweet and refreshing, with a mustardy bite. Although it's a brassica, kohlrabi grows like fennel, just above the ground. Suitable swaps: fennel, radishes or apple.

Lamb's lettuce

Also known as mâche or corn salad, lamb's lettuce is a delicate salad leaf that's surprisingly hardy, growing right through the winter. Visually, the leaves looks like watercress yet the flavour is delicate. Suitable swaps: purslane or Little Gem lettuce.

Pak choi

This attractive vegetable, with dark green leaves and pale stems, has the same reviving freshness as cabbage. Use small pak choi leaves whole in salads, or finely shred denser

leaves and stems. Either way, pak choi is a delicious addition to Green beans, five-spice crispy duck and bean sprouts (page 176). Suitable swaps: Little Gem lettuce, fennel or cabbage.

Pears

A gem of the orchard, pears provide a creamy texture and a delicious, honeyed diversion to peppery leaves and earthy roots. Try adding a little diced pear to Lentils, mustard, watercress and parsley (page 122) for a fruity foil. Firmer pears are also brilliant pickled (see page 83), giving you an instant boost for simple leafy salads throughout the year. Suitable swaps: apples or plums.

Peppers

Charred sweet peppers are a favourite in my salads. They are particularly good in Leftover lamb, harissa and char-grilled peppers (page 155). Char an extra couple of peppers for this recipe and serve as a simple salad the next day, tossed with chopped parsley, Little Gem lettuce leaves, olive oil and Marcona (or simple toasted) almonds. Suitable swaps: tomatoes or roasted aubergines.

Plums

Hugh loves pairing plums with tomatoes. Visually, when diced and tossed together in a simple drizzle of olive oil with a pinch of salt and some spices or herbs, they camouflage one another, making each bite a bit of a surprise – one is sweet, the other tangy. They are also great roasted or raw in a salad of peppery leaves with a creamy goat's cheese, burrata or nuggets of blue cheese, like Blue Vinny. Suitable swaps: greengages or damsons.

Pumpkins and squashes

King of the autumn garden, Crown Prince has to be one of my favourite squash varieties. Its dense flesh has a rich, chestnut-y flavour that pairs well with spice. Chunks of roasted squash feature in several recipes (see pages 138, 163 and 172). You could also add them to

Spicy, nutty quinoa (page 141), or use them in place of the winter veg in Curried roots, pearled barley and parsley (page 77) for an autumnal twist. Suitable swaps: sweet potatoes or carrots.

Radicchio

An Italian classic, radicchio is a late-autumn, early-winter head of beautiful, white-veined red leaves. It has a bitter, spicy taste, which mellows beautifully when grilled or roasted. You would never know it, but this veg is in the sunflower family along with artichokes (globe and Jerusalem). Radicchio – raw or roasted – is brilliant paired with citrus or orchard fruits, like pears, as well as nuts and seeds. The leaves are also lovely shredded and folded through creamy haricot beans (see page 134), or tossed into Roast squash, blackberries, feta and walnuts (page 172). Suitable swap: chicory.

WINTER

Brussels sprouts

If you think of Brussels sprouts as miniature cabbages, their role as a salad ingredient snaps into place. They work brilliantly finely shredded in wintry slaws, such as my Brussels sprout Waldorf (page 190), where they are paired with apples, Cheddar and walnuts. You can also ferment them by weaving shreds of Brussels through the Kimkraut (page 232). Another great way to enjoy them is roasted – try swapping them for the cauliflower florets in Roast cauliflower with pumpkin seed satay (page 137). Suitable swaps: cabbage or cauliflower florets.

Celeriac

Creamy and nutty with a celery edge to the flavour, celeriac must be one of my favourite roots to feature in salads. I love it raw, cut into batons, grated or finely diced. It partners well with unexpected ingredients like forced rhubarb, or oily fish such as sardines and mackerel. Suitable swaps: celery or parsnips.

Celery

Punchier and crunchier than celeriac, celery works well with strong, creamy ingredients as a refreshing foil. Thin slivery moons are delicious in my Potato salad with apples and Cheddar (page 196). Or cut celery into batons and add – either raw or roasted until golden – to Lentils with green herbs and lemon (page 160). Suitable swaps: celeriac or rhubarb.

Chicory

Crunchy and refreshing with a bitter edge, radicchio's smaller cousin can be rouge-hued or a mellow yellow. As with radicchio, it's great with fruit – try Grilled pears and chicory with toasted walnuts (page 119), or Swede, sprouts, chestnuts and char-grilled clementines (page 78). Suitable swaps: radicchio or watercress.

Jerusalem artichokes

Creamy, nutty and full of prebiotic benefits, Jerusalem artichokes taste like a root veg version of hazelnuts. They are, in fact, tubers in the sunflower family and the prebiotic bit can sometimes cause digestive disruption: the artichokes feed the good bacteria in your gut and that feeding frenzy can lead to ... er, gas. But it's worth shaving raw slivers or roasting nuggets of Jerusalem artichokes to add to salads – they're lovely paired with winter leaves, fresh thyme, lemon and my creamy almond dressing on page 114. Suitable swaps: parsnips or salsify.

Kale

Stripped from their woody stalks, hearty kale leaves soften into moreish winter salad leaves when massaged with a little salt and olive oil. I love partnering them with seasonal fruit, particularly apples in autumn and winter (see page 74). During the summer, young kale leaves are lovely paired with peaches and cheese – anything from a delicate, ashy goat's cheese to a punchy blue (see page 97). You can also roast oiled and salted kale leaves to add a leafy crunch to salads. Suitable swap: hispi cabbage leaves.

Leeks

While spring onions are the more obvious salad companion, leeks – finely shredded and roasted until crisp – make a brilliant crunchy salad topping. They are also delicious halved lengthways and barbecued (see page 91). And you can toss shredded leeks through ferments and pickles for a tangy, oniony kick. Suitable swaps: spring onions, shallots, red or white onions.

Parsnips

Treat parsnips like celeriac, albeit a sweeter, more carroty version, and you've got a brilliant addition to your salad-making armoury. They work well raw and grated as the star of the show. Or, introduce parsnip as a backup singer to a rooty slaw alongside beetroot, carrots and celeriac with spices – toss with the merguez spice blend on page 138, and a light dressing made with fresh orange juice and rapeseed oil. Suitable swaps: celeriac or carrots.

Swede

A member of the brassica family, this root has the subtle sweetness of carrot (or squash) married with the mustardy spice of cabbage or Brussels sprouts. In moderation, it works well grated and raw, with spice and toasted seeds, but I prefer it diced, roasted and woven into the mix like a spicy rooty croûton. Suitable swaps: celeriac or Brussels sprouts (halved or quartered).

Turnips

Flavourwise, creamy, peppery, fresh turnips are a delicious cross between radishes and kohlrabi. Do use them in place of, or in addition to, the kohlrabi in the slaw on page 189. Young turnips are also wonderful thinly sliced 'carpaccio-style' and used as a base for leaves or other salads to sit upon. Suitable swaps: radishes or kohlrabi.

Grow your own salad

There's no denying that growing your own salad leaves – and other ingredients, too, if you've got the space – will give you the tastiest salads, by far. Homegrown salads also have a greater concentration of nutrients, and they can be a lot cheaper. Another boon is a reduction in food miles and environmentally unfriendly packaging – so many commercially produced salads still come housed in plastic.

Growing your own salad leaves is surprisingly easy and you don't need a garden – in fact, you don't even need a window box. Below are a few homegrown salad projects you can do at your kitchen table. They're great to get kids involved with, too – it's often a cunning ploy to entice them to eat more of the good stuff, as engaging in the growing process gives them more motivation to get stuck in.

TABLETOP SALAD POTS

You can literally grow salad leaves on your kitchen table. While you do need some sunlight, there are several varieties which you can grow that will spring to life quickly, even in the depths of winter, in small spaces with basic materials.

Pea shoots

Nutty and sweet, pea shoots taste like leafy versions of podded peas, and like the pods, the shoots are rich in Vitamins C and A, and protein. Growing pea shoots is the perfect entry-level gardening project. They only need one or two hours of sun a day and you can reap the rewards in a week or so.

What you need
- Dried peas: Those sold for cooking will normally grow fine and are much cheaper than buying seed packets
- A 6–9cm deep waterproof tray or container
- Organic, peat-free compost

How to grow
First, soak the peas in cold water for 24 hours.

Select a suitable container. Find a 6–9cm deep waterproof tray or other container with holes in the bottom to allow water to drain out. The trays sold in gardening stores for seed-growing are perfect.

Fill your container with compost, to about 2cm from the top, then give the compost a good water.

Sow the seeds on top of the compost. You can sow them very close together but it's better to leave a gap the size of a pea between each seed.

Cover the seeds with a layer of compost, about the thickness of a pea. Water the surface lightly again.

Check daily for watering. Your goal now is simply to keep the compost moist – check it every day in hot weather, every couple of days in cooler weather, and water when needed.

Harvest and enjoy! In just two weeks (a bit longer in cold weather) the crop will have grown 6–7cm tall. Your pea shoots are now ready to harvest and eat. Harvest by pinching off each shoot just above the bottom leaves.

Some of the pea shoots may regrow to give you a second crop.

Recipes featuring pea shoots
- Peppery leaves with kohlrabi and melon (page 66)
- Fennel, celery and apple with creamy almond dressing (page 114)

Wild rocket

A spicy hit of pepper is the distinctive trademark of these addictive (in my mind), accessible leaves. They are rich in chlorophyll, which helps protect our cells from damage caused by environmental toxins and the ageing process – a definite benefit!

Wild rocket is easy to grow and in just 3–4 weeks from sowing you can be harvesting baby leaves for your salads. Or if you plant these outdoors in the spring, you'll have a full-blown rocket patch in a couple of months, which will come back year after year. Key for larger leaves is to give them as much sun exposure as possible – if there's not enough light, the leaves may turn yellowish.

What you need
- Wild rocket seeds
- A 6–9cm deep waterproof tray or container for rocket shoots. Opt for a deeper tray (12–16cm) to establish larger rocket leaves for indoors or to transplant outdoors
- Organic, peat-free compost. If you can, mix it with a few handfuls of perlite or vermiculite (both are volcanic materials which help with drainage); heat-treated rice husks are a great organic alternative

How to grow
Select a suitable container. For smaller rocket leaves, a 6–9cm deep waterproof tray (such as a seed tray) or similar container is perfect, or opt for a deeper (12–16cm) tray, trug or pot for larger leaves. Key is to ensure the container has holes in the bottom to allow the water to drain out.

Fill your container with compost, to about 2cm from the top, then give it a good water.

Sow by sprinkling a dusting of seeds on top of the compost. You can sow them very close together if you're just growing small leaves, but for larger ones, space the seeds 1cm apart.

Cover the seeds with a 1cm deep layer of compost. Pat the compost down over the seeds, then water the surface lightly again.

Check daily for watering. Your goal now is simply to keep the compost moist. Check it every day in hot weather, every couple of days in cooler weather, and water when needed.

Harvest and enjoy! In around 3 weeks (a bit longer in cold weather) you'll have a carpet of mini rocket leaves (4–5cm high), or if you leave them for another 2–3 weeks you'll have fully grown leaves (8–10cm tall) to harvest or transplant into your garden. Cut or pick the salad leaves from the plant as and when they are needed. Picking leaves regularly will ensure that plenty of tasty new leaves keep growing.

Recipes featuring rocket
- Leftover roast beef with rocket and horseradish crème fraîche (page 69)
- Barley, rocket pesto, Cheddar and chives (page 166)
- Grilled pears and chicory with toasted walnuts (page 119)

Bean (and other) sprouts

Sprouting pulses, beans, grains, nuts and seeds not only helps you transform something dormant from your kitchen cupboard into a nutrient-rich, living food, it's also an easy and cheap way to create delicious ingredients to boost the health benefits, texture and taste of your salads.

On the health front, sprouts are one of the most nutritionally dense foods you can eat, containing up to 30 per cent more protein than their unsprouted and cooked counterparts and up to 10 times more B vitamins, immune-supporting vitamin C and calcium. They're also much easier to digest.

What you need
- A handful of dried mung beans (or other things you can sprout, see below)
- 1 tbsp cider vinegar
- A glass bowl or measuring jug
- A fine-meshed sieve
- A clean tea towel

How to sprout
Soak the beans: Place them in a glass bowl or jug and cover with plenty of water (3–4 times the volume of what you're soaking). Add 1 tbsp cider vinegar to the water. Cover with a clean tea towel and leave at room temperature for 24 hours (see below for other soaking times).

Drain and keep damp: Tip the beans into a sieve, wash with cold water and drain as many times as it takes for the water to become clear. Then sit the sieve over a bowl to help aerate the beans. Dampen your cloth with water and place it over the sieve to keep your budding sprouts moist. This will create a humid but well-aerated environment for them to sprout.

Rinse the sprouts 2 or 3 times a day until they being to sprout a rootlet. This keeps them moist; the rinsing also prevents them from harbouring bacteria. The combination of light, moisture and air will help the beans to sprout.

Harvest and enjoy! In just 1–4 days, your sprouted beans should be ready (see below for other sprouting times). Eat within 2–3 days. Store in the fridge.

Other things you can sprout
- **Almonds** 12 hours soaking, 12 hours sprouting
- **Barley** 7 hours soaking, 2 days sprouting
- **Broccoli seeds** 4 hours soaking, 2 days sprouting
- **Buckwheat** 15 minutes soaking, 1–2 days sprouting
- **Chickpeas** 12 hours soaking, 12 hours sprouting
- **Lentils** 8 hours soaking, 12 hours sprouting
- **Oats (whole)** 6 hours soaking, 2–3 days sprouting
- **Pumpkin seeds** 12 hours soaking, 2–3 days sprouting
- **Quinoa** 2 hours soaking, 1–2 days sprouting
- **Spelt** 8 hours soaking, 2–3 days sprouting
- **Sunflower seeds** 2 hours soaking, 2–3 days sprouting

Recipes featuring bean sprouts
- Crispy fried sumac squid, pak choi and bean sprouts (page 125)
- Sticky beef, bean sprouts and coriander (page 99)
- For variety and a nutritional boost, swap out cooked quinoa, spelt or lentils, or raw almonds, in recipes for the sprouted version

Microgreens
Microgreens are the first shoots of edible plants that include the stem, the cotyledons (or seed leaves) and the first set of true leaves, i.e. the first 5–6cm of growth of a plant.

Sometimes referred to as 'vegetable confetti', microgreens take in a variety of veg, including alfalfa, broccoli, kale, spinach and watercress, as well as herbs such as basil, coriander, dill, and parsley. Not only do microgreens add visual appeal and zest to a plate of food, they also give an intense flavour boost, and enrich the health profile of any salad enormously, offering essential nutrients. Beyond the benefits, microgreens are also easy to grow at home – even in your own kitchen.

What you need
- Seeds: It's best to start with one type of seed, such as broccoli, radish, red cabbage, kale, pak choi, rocket or coriander – these are all easy to grow in a single container. Then progress to growing a combination of different varieties
- A 6–9cm deep waterproof tray or container (or you can buy a kit with seeds and containers online at teenygreeny.co.uk)
- Organic, peat-free compost. If you can, mix it with a few handfuls of perlite or vermiculite (both are volcanic materials which help with drainage); heat-treated rice husks are a great organic alternative

How to grow

Find a space and container: Start with a warm, sunny windowsill (direct sunlight from a south-facing window is ideal) and a small, clean container. Plastic take-away dishes and disposable pie plates work well, as do clear fruit or salad punnets. If your chosen container doesn't have built-in drainage, poke a few drainage holes in the bottom.

Prepare your seeds and soil: Read the seed packet to see if there are any special instructions. Cover the bottom of the container with a 3–5cm depth of moistened potting compost or mix. Flatten and level it with your hand or a small piece of cardboard, taking care not to over-compress the compost.

Sow your seeds by scattering them evenly on top of the compost. Press gently into the compost using your hand or the cardboard. Cover the seeds with a thin layer of soil. Dampen the surface, using a mister. If you prefer, you can skip this step and instead cover the container with a clear lid until the seeds are sprouted.

Keep the compost moist, warm and exposed to light. While waiting for sprouts to appear, usually within 3 to 7 days, use the mister once or twice daily to keep the soil moist but not wet. Once seeds have sprouted, remove the cover (if you've used one) and continue to mist once or twice a day.

Microgreens need about 4 hours direct sunlight every day to thrive. In winter months, when the sun isn't as strong, some may need even more. Leggy, pale greens are a sign of insufficient sunlight. Light needs can also be satisfied with a grow light.

Harvesting: Depending upon the type of seeds you've selected, your microgreens will be ready to harvest about 2–3 weeks after planting. Look for the first set of true leaves as a sign of readiness. Then grab your scissors and snip the greens just above the soil line.

To serve, wash the microgreens with water and dry with kitchen paper or a salad spinner. Serve immediately for the freshest flavour or store briefly in a lidded container in the fridge.

Adding microgreens to recipes

All the salads in this book will benefit from a finishing touch of microgreens. Here are a few specific suggestions:

- Red cabbage, apple, sauerkraut and parsley (page 46); add red cabbage microgreens in addition to the red cabbage
- Seedy kale and kimchi with orange and seaweed dressing (page 56); add kale microgreens in addition or in place of the full-grown kale leaves
- Barbecued leeks, spelt and sunflower seeds (page 91); add sunflower microgreens in addition to the sunflower seeds
- Broccoli with chilli and pumpkin seeds (page 142); use coriander microgreens in place of the full-grown coriander
- Green beans, five-spice crispy duck and bean sprouts (page 176); add pak choi microgreens

MIXED LEAF CONTAINER GARDEN

You can grow a myriad of salad leaves nestled together in a large container, window box or grow-bag, offering you tasty, instant-access salad leaves year-round. The key is to find a sunny spot near a window, a good outdoor window box spot, a sunny patio space or patch of soil in a garden or allotment.

Once you've got your space sorted, salad leaves grow within just 30–40 days of planting. For the price of a bag of salad leaves, you can buy a pack of seeds that could keep you in lettuce year-round for a couple of years. Here are my favourite cut-and-come-again varieties, inspired by what we grow at River Cottage and what I love to eat.

Plant these varieties and you will a have tasty mingling of frolicky flavoursome leaves, with a variety of shapes, colours and textures for all your salad-making needs. Plant a selection (or all ten) or seek out a seed mix containing some of these delicious leaves.

Claytonia
Sometimes called miner's lettuce, Claytonia is typically used in winter salads and is one of the hardiest salad crops available. It has heart-shaped, slightly succulent leaves, with a mild flavour. Both the leaves and flowering shoots can be eaten.

Kale, blue
This variety of kale is similar to the richer purple Russian kale but is lighter in hue and texture, making it a great leafy option for salads throughout the year.

Mizuna
A Japanese leafy vegetable that grows as a large rosette of feathery leaves with a peppery, cabbage flavour. It lends a bit of bite and heat to salads.

Mustard greens
Related to kale, cabbage and collard greens, these are the leaves of the mustard plant and are used frequently in Chinese, Japanese and Indian cooking. They're less bitter than kale or collard greens, and more peppery, like rocket.

Great varieties include Ruby Streaks and Red Zest for spring/summer sowing, and Red Lace and Green Frills in the winter.

Orach
Light green, leafy orach is ideal for all-season growing. It doesn't get bitter when it begins to bolt, unlike lettuce.

Pak choi
A member of the cabbage family, this mild leaf can be grown and harvested when it's still small and bite-sized. It has a number of different names, including Chinese celery cabbage and white mustard cabbage.

Golden Yellow and Canton White are two varieties to seek out.

Perpetual spinach
This prolific green leafy vegetable is very similar in taste and texture to spinach and is often sold as chard. It's an underrated and worthwhile plant to grow, particularly for those with a tiny garden or those with no time. Just shove it in and it will produce spinach leaves for an entire year.

Perpetual Erbette, Bright Lights and Early Prickly are great varieties.

Sorrel
More often classified as a herb, sorrel is well worth growing as a salad leaf for its tangy, lip-puckering lemon flavour. For salads, you really need to use young and tender leaves. Sorrel is known to permaculturists as a dynamic accumulator cover crop, which, in simple terms, means it's great for feeding the soil and your other plants.

Lemon sorrel, Buckler-leaved and red-veined sorrel are all good varieties to grow.

Rocket

This peppery leaf, also known as arugula, is a great addition to salads. Wild rocket with its sharply serrated leaves and salad rocket are the varieties to plant. Quick-growing, yet refined, with good vigour and uniformity, they add so much texture and flavour to any salad.

Yukina Savoy

The thick, dark green, shiny, spoon-shaped leaves of this plant grow upright and look like a larger version of tatsoi. Vigorous and easy to grow, heat and cold resistant, Yukina Savoy can be grown year-round. Harvest the leaves young for a mild flavour. They are a great addition to salad mixes.

What you need to grow salad leaves

- Seeds: Choose from the above varieties
- Organic, peat-free compost. Spending a little more on a good organic, peat-free compost will pay you in healthier and more abundant leaves. Carbon Gold's Biochar all-purpose compost (or similar) is a great choice – it's very light, so it doesn't add weight to your windowsill, and absorbent so you don't have to water so often
- Perlite, vermiculite or heat-treated rice husks to mix with your compost. Mixing a few handfuls in creates a compost blend with good drainage
- Plant food: For your salad leaves to grow strong, they need a nitrogen-rich feed added to the soil every couple of weeks. Two options are a seaweed-based feed (which is vegan/vegetarian-friendly) or an organic garden fertiliser that is made from fish

How to grow

Choose your seeds: Buy individually or look out for seed mixes, which can be more economical. You can often get spring/summer and autumn/winter seed blends.

Find the right spot: A sunny windowsill or conservatory is an easy, successful solution for year-round growing. If you want to grow your leaves outdoors, you can start sowing from mid spring through to late summer or do both – a container inside and a patch outside.

Start sowing: You can either sow different types in individual rows or pots, or simply sprinkle a salad-leaf seed mix on a patch of bare soil or a compost-filled container. Most salad seed is very small and need only be sown in very shallow drills, covered with a thin layer of compost. A depth no greater than the width of your little finger is suitable.

Watering the soil before sowing will help ensure seeds are in close contact with moist soil, rather than watering the row afterwards. In garden soil, where there may be weed seeds present, it's better to sow in rows so that germinated salad seedlings can be easily distinguished from weeds.

Once you've planted your seeds, cover them with a 1cm layer of compost, pat down and water. To ensure the longest, steadiest supply of young leaves throughout the growing season, try to sow small batches of seed every 2 weeks until late August.

Water and wait: Keep your soil and seeds well hydrated with a regular supply of water. Ensure you pull out any weeds in between rows if growing outdoors.

Harvest: It is best to harvest salad leaves in the morning when they are at their most succulent. Snip the leaves about 2.5cm from the base. Avoid damaging the central growing point of the plant and allow the remaining leaves to grow on.

Try to only harvest what you will use each day, as baby leaves can wilt quickly. If you need to store them, dampen the leaves and put them into a sealed container in the salad drawer of the fridge.

Nurture your plants for a continuous supply of leaves. Water regularly to help support the production of new leaves. Each sowing should give you three or four cuts before the plants are exhausted.

Many plants will become tough, bitter or try to flower and should then be lifted, composted and the ground fed with fresh compost or a liquid feed and re-sown.

LETTUCE FOR ALL SEASONS

Growing heads of lettuce is a little more challenging than faster-growing salad leaves but it's deliciously satisfying and far cheaper than buying them. You also avoid all that environmentally unfriendly packaging.

Lettuces come in a wide variety of shapes, colours and textures, and the array you can grow is far greater than the choice of shop-bought lettuces. Here, I'm listing some of my favourite varieties. Add them to the salads in the book or create a simple side salad by tossing freshly harvested lettuce leaves with one of the dressings in the final chapter (see pages 215–226).

Green Batavia

A classic summer cut-and-come again variety with crinkled leaves that are sweet and crisp. Batavia was the precursor to the less tasty Iceberg lettuce and makes a great swap for Cos in salads. Sow in the spring to harvest through the summer.

Little Gem

This great all-rounder is used throughout the book, so why not try growing a few of your own. It's a brilliant choice for so many things – both raw and cooked. Little Gem is actually a type of Cos lettuce and it delivers on that cool crisp hit, but is much easier to grow outdoors than a true Cos.

Lollo Rosso

Also known as red coral lettuce because of its beautiful, tight curled leaves, this familiar lettuce has a deep earthy flavour. If you soak it in a bowl of cold water with 1 tsp each salt and cider vinegar for around half an hour the leaves will become even more crisp and delicious. It has a very close relation called Lollo Bionda, which has paler green leaves, so consider planting both for a variety of colours.

Merveille de Quatre Saisons

A winter lettuce to sow in the autumn, this is an old variety with a big, open structure and beautiful, crumpled bronze outer leaves for picking almost all year.

Radicchio

Again, this features in several recipes in the book and you'll get a more intense flavour from home grown. It's a type of perennial chicory with deep red leaves that have white veins and stems. Radicchio grows well in the slightly cooler months, plugging a gap where other softer lettuces struggle to thrive.

Reine de Glaces

This is a crisphead variety of summer lettuce with a relaxed, open growing habit, producing a small green centre surrounded by looser outer leaves with spiky, lacy edges. Sow it in the spring to harvest individually through the summer months.

Rosalita

A summer lettuce rosette with red-tipped leaves with a refreshing crunch. The variety is relatively heat resistant should summer bring a hot spell, and it's slow to bolt.

Rouge d'Hiver

This Romaine-style lettuce is an extremely beautiful 1800s European heirloom variety. Its large, flat, broad leaves are sweet, with a delicious buttery texture. The colour varies from green through bronze to deep red. It's a quick-growing lettuce and cold resistant. Sow in the autumn for a winter crop.

Winter Butterhead

This versatile, reliable butterhead variety is ideal for successional sowings throughout the year. Medium heads with solid, crisp hearts are produced from hardy reliable plants, even in dry weather. Autumn sowings should be grown under cloches or in a cold greenhouse for over-wintering but can be harvested in spring for early salads.

What you need

- Seeds: Choose from the varieties described on page 30
- Organic, peat-free compost. It's worth buying a good all-purpose compost, such as Carbon Gold's Biochar
- Perlite, vermiculite or heat-treated rice husks to mix with your compost – to create good drainage
- Plant food: For your lettuces to grow strong, they need a nitrogen-rich feed added to the soil every couple of weeks. Two options are a seaweed-based feed (which is vegan/vegetarian-friendly) or an organic garden fertiliser that is made from fish

How to grow lettuces

Prepare your soil by digging in lots of well-rotted garden compost beforehand. This helps to prevent lettuces bolting or running to seed in hot or dry weather, especially in light soils.

Sow your seeds on moist, well-prepared soil or compost in spring for summer lettuces, or autumn for over-wintering lettuces (to harvest late autumn and then over-winter for spring harvesting).

Use a bamboo cane to press a 1cm deep trench in the soil then moisten the soil. Sow the seeds thinly in the trench. Leave 30cm between rows. Cover seeds thinly with soil or vermiculite – they germinate better if they get some light.

If sowing in pots, scatter seed sparingly over the surface of moist, peat-free seed compost and cover with a fine layer of compost or vermiculite.

Thin the seedlings out to 10–20cm apart when they are big enough to handle. (You can use the thinnings in a salad.) Water along the row to resettle the soil around the roots of the remaining plants.

Don't let the soil get too dry, especially if the weather is hot, or the crop will bolt (run to seed). Early- and late-season sowings are less inclined to bolt.

If you're growing lettuces in a container, water from the bottom up. Sit the box in a large container of water – a bath will do – and when the top surface turns damp you'll know the entire box has been watered. If you would rather water from the top, make sure you keep going until water starts to come out of the drainage holes.

Mulch the area around your lettuces to seal moisture into the soil and feed your plants. Keep the area around the plants weed-free.

Protect from pests, especially slugs and snails, which can literally decimate your crop. Use copper-impregnated matting, or mulch the soil with sharp grit or crushed eggshells or seashells. Red or purple lettuces seem to be less prone to attack.

Protect your plants from weather. Downy mildew fungus can ruin a crop. This is a particular problem in wet weather towards the end of the summer. Avoid splashing the leaves when watering and space the plants far enough apart to ensure there is good circulation of air.

Start picking baby loose-leaf lettuces at 6 weeks, or at 10 weeks for hearting types. They're best harvested in the early morning, before the leaves dehydrate in the sun. The key tip when harvesting lettuce leaves is to make a clean cut using a knife or scissors. Most greens will re-grow after cutting if you leave about 2cm of plant behind. Individual leaves may be picked, entire heads may be cut, or cutting mixes and leaf lettuce may be cropped off with scissors.

For a steady supply of lettuces, sow seed every couple of weeks from March through to September.

HERBS FOR SALADS

Having a few pots of herbs to hand will give you instant flavour pops for your salads, and you can house plants inside if you don't have outdoor space. As well as boosting the culinary experience of a salad – taste-wise, aromatically and visually – herbs will also give it an additional health kick. These are some of my favourite salad herbs.

Basil

Depending on the variety, basil's flavour profile can stretch from peppery feistiness, through subtle mint to fennel-like aniseed. Good salad varieties include Cinnamon, Dark Opal, Greek, Lemon and Sweet Genovese. The nutty seed heads are great in salads too.

Try basil in: Cucumber, grapes, apple and almond (page 52)

Chervil

One of the French *fines herbes*, chervil has a lacy texture and tastes like a toned-down, delicate mingling of tarragon and parsley.

Try chervil in: Parsnip, chicory, orange and prunes (page 62)

Chives

The perfect partner for potatoes, chives have a mild, grassy flavour similar to baby spring onions or wild garlic. Use the flowers, broken into little pops of purple confetti, as well as the green stems, finely snipped.

Try chives in: Roast cauliflower with pumpkin seed satay (page 137)

Coriander

This versatile herb is related to parsley, carrots and celery, yet the flavour is punchy and citrussy. We grow it all year round at River Cottage – in the polytunnel in the winter and out in the garden throughout the summer. Coriander pairs surprisingly well with root veg.

Try coriander in: Dhal salad (page 171)

Dill

A green herb with tender, thread-like leaves, which grow in clusters, dill has a strong, distinctive taste that is like a combination of fennel and celery, with warm, slightly bitter undertones.

Try dill in: Roast squash, blackberries, feta and walnuts (page 172)

Fennel

Bronze fennel and other fennel herb varieties are related to the vegetable, Florence fennel, but without the bulb. The feathery leaves have the same aroma and flavour, and as the year ebbs toward autumn you get tall heads of delicious yellow flowers followed by juicy green seeds that dry to brown. Every part of the plant has the distinctive, aniseed-like aroma and taste, and can be used in salads to give an aromatic lift.

Try fennel in: Apple with toasted hazelnuts and lime (page 113)

Lemon balm

A common weed in most people's garden, the leaves look like a cross between nettle and mint – but the flavour is more akin to lemon verbena, yet milder. The leaves are soft and add a delicate citrussy flavour to salads.

Try lemon balm in: Peas, mint, Oakleaf lettuce and grapes (page 108)

Lemon verbena

Lending a punchy lemongrass edge, lemon verbena can be a lovely zingy addition to all manner of summer salads.

Try lemon verbena in: Beetroot, sea bass, blackberries and chilli (page 153)

Lovage

I like to think of lovage as an intensified, herbaceous version of celery. It's surprisingly good with rhubarb and goat's cheese in a simple salad – dressed with olive oil and finished with toasted hazelnuts.

Try lovage in: Grilled pears and chicory with toasted walnuts (page 119)

Mint

Aromatic and lifting on so many levels, classic Moroccan mint and any milder, softer leaved versions are great in salads – as opposed to more velvety varieties like apple mint or punchy numbers like spearmint.

Try mint in: Blackberries, pear, apple and oats (page 58)

Oregano

Our bees love feasting on the nectar from this deeply savoury, velvety-leafed herb, which is brilliant with everything from tomatoes to celeriac. You wouldn't know it by taste but this herb is a member of the mint family. I like to use it as a flavour boost in salads.

Try oregano in: Fennel with chilli, lemon and dill (page 144)

Parsley

The two main groups of parsley used as herbs are French (or curly leaf) and the Italian, or flat-leaf parsley. Of these, flat-leaf more closely resembles the natural wild species. It will enhance almost any salad, adding a lovely fresh green back note.

Try parsley in: Spiced spelt salad with apples and lime (page 132)

Sage

Crispy, lightly fried sage leaves make a brilliant, savoury herbaceous alternative to croûtons in a salad. Very fine slivers of sage woven through grainy salads also work well.

Try sage in: Barley tabbouleh (page 187)

Sorrel

With a refreshing, lemony taste, sorrel will give a sour smack to any salad. It's a lovely leaf – especially the red-veined variety. The young leaves are particularly good in a fish salad.

Try sorrel in: Smoked Mackerel niçoise (page 203)

Tarragon

The aniseed-flavoured leaves of French tarragon are great with lentils, radishes, broad beans, apples, kohlrabi and so much more.

Try tarragon in: Charred courgettes, broad beans, mangetout and fresh curds (page 88)

Thyme

Fresh thyme leaves add colour and an aromatic lift to winter root salads. The herb is particularly good with salads featuring celeriac and carrots.

Try thyme in: French dressing (page 219)

Winter savory

A perennial, semi-evergreen, which looks and tastes a lot like thyme, but with slightly more elongated, dark green leaves. In the summer it produces pale lavender flowers, which are delicious and attractive in salads. Winter savory is a great foil to sweet winter roots, spicy flavours and cabbage.

Try winter savory in: Carrot, cabbage, ginger and chilli slaw (page 198)

How to grow

Most herbs thrive in full sun, in a sheltered position. You can grow herbs indoors on the windowsill, in pots outdoors or straight in the ground. Sow seeds of annual herbs like basil and coriander every couple of weeks to provide you with fresh leaves throughout the summer.

Plant perennial herbs such as oregano, rosemary, chives and mint in pots or in the ground and harvest the leaves as and when you need them. Save seeds from annual herbs at the end of the year, and keep your perennial herbs in the ground as they'll grow again the following year.

How to harvest

You can harvest herbs as needed through the growing season, once there is enough foliage on the plant to support growth. Snipping the plants regularly helps to encourage new growth and keep the herbs healthy. Limit these harvests to less than one-third of the plant so it keeps growing and producing more foliage. The ideal time to harvest most herbs for the best flavour is early in the morning right after the dew has dried, but before the sun's rays evaporate the aromatic oils.

Annual herbs Harvest leafy, annual herbs like basil and marjoram by pinching off leaves from the tips of the stems right above a pair of leaves. The plant will sprout two branches above the leaves and continue to grow. This is also called 'pinching out' and encourages the plant to become bushy and produce more tender foliage. Harvest leafy tips frequently and clip off flower buds to keep the plant producing. Harvest the entire plant before your first frost.

Perennial herbs Varieties such as thyme, sage and tarragon can be harvested by the stem or sprig. Cut the stems 7–10cm from the base of the plant. Harvest herbs with long stems like parsley and oregano by cutting the stem near the base of the plant. Harvest rosemary by cutting stems above a pair of leaves and it will branch out and continue to grow.

Continue to harvest perennial herbs until around 4 weeks before you expect your first frost. As winter approaches, allow the plant to focus on winding down for the season before going dormant.

Herb blossoms Some herbs have single flowers, like rosemary, while others present their blooms in clusters, like fennel, coriander and dill. Single blossoms are best harvested by picking the individual flowers when the flower is opened fully. Clusters of blossom are best harvested when some of the flowers are open, by cutting the stem 10–12cm from the base of the plant or just above the top set of leaves.

Herb seeds You can also allow herbs to go to seed for harvest, such as fennel, coriander and dill. It's best to leave them to dry on the plant. Allow the herb to form flowers and go to seed. After flowering, seeds swell and ripen from green to brown or black as they dry. Seeds are ready to pick when they are dry.

FLOWERS

Another way to give your salads added colour, flavour and, in some instances, fragrance, is the addition of edible flowers. Some of my favourites are borage, calendula, cornflower, dianthus, nasturtiums, pansies, tagetes and violas. They make an attractive finishing flourish, or you can mix them with lettuce leaves and herbs to turn a simple salad into something more spectacular.

WILD LEAVES

Wild leaves have strong, pronounced flavours and can be an excellent addition to salads, or you can forage a seasonal mix to create a salad comprised solely of wild leaves to marry with one of the dressings in the final chapter (see pages 215–226).

Gathering wild leaves (and flowers – of which there are plenty) is not only deeply satisfying (and free) it also makes for some of the most nourishing salads you can eat, and it's the perfect way to embrace a local, seasonal approach to eating.

Some of my favourite wild finds are: chickweed (leaves and flowers), dandelion (leaves and flowers), elderflowers, hairy bittercress, horseradish leaves, mallow (leaves and flowers), salad burnet, sorrel, wild garlic (leaves and flowers) and wood sorrel (leaves and flowers).

When you're foraging for wild ingredients, never gather more than a third of what is there – you want to ensure there is plenty to regenerate and enough for wildlife to feast on as well. Always wash your foraged finds and try not to pick from places where dogs pee, or where local councils might spray (such as local parks). If you ever spot a patch of yellow grass, it's probably because the council are spraying to kill the weeds you fancy foraging.

So always be careful, know the land you're harvesting from and be sure you're certain of what you're harvesting.

Salad techniques

While the quality of your ingredients is by far the most important marker for achieving salad success, the way you prepare your ingredients is definitely next on the list. You can completely transform the eating experience by char-grilling fruit to add to the mix, or grating root veg you'd never considered eating raw, or creating a tangle of veg ribbons to nestle nuggets of crumbled goat's cheese, herbs and toasted buckwheat groats. Here are some of the techniques covered in the book, with a raft of variations you can try in other recipes, or use to create your own salads, employing the seasonal veg and fruit you have to hand at any given time.

CHAR-GRILLING AND BARBECUING

A magical transformation happens when you cook vegetables and fruits over (or under) an intense heat, which is called the Maillard reaction. It is a form of browning that develops when naturally occurring sugars reduce, losing water, and react with the amino acids in the food, intensifying the flavours significantly. It also results in a richer texture, while often retaining a hint of raw, refreshing crunch. These things are somewhat unexpected when it comes to salads, which makes it all the more fun to weave charred, grilled and barbecued vegetables – and fruits – into your repertoire.

You can probably detect my love of charred veg in salads from the recipes they feature in, which are peppered throughout the book (see pages 78, 83, 88, 91, 119 and 155).

Once you've tried these, you can take the concept and apply the technique to ingredients in some of the other salad recipes which might feature the veg raw or roasted, for added fun, variety and to shake things up. Asparagus, broccoli, chicory, courgettes, fennel, leeks, peppers, squash, tomatoes and pears are particularly successful.

ROASTING

Beyond the more direct contact with heat, the difference between char-grilled (or barbecued) and roasted veg is that when you roast the veg (or fruit) in the oven there's an element of steam circulating, which cooks your ingredients more and keeps everything deliciously moist.

Roasting encapsulates all those sticky, sweet edges created by the caramelisation of sugars, but over a slower period. The slower cooking and retention of moisture give you flavour-rich roasted ingredients with a crispy outside and a tender centre that are easy to eat and totally delicious. All of the veg and fruit that respond well to char-grilling and barbecuing (see left) are excellent roasted, and many more besides, notably potatoes, all root veg, apples and rhubarb.

Roasted veg work beautifully with lots of fresh herbs, raw crispy salad leaves and/or grains and pulses. You'll find my favourite roasted salad recipes on pages 93, 104, 137, 138, 172 and 221, but of course, you can swap things around and mix and match the cooking techniques in the different recipes to see how a slightly different approach can alter the eating experience.

RAW VEG

You can add textural interest to salads by preparing raw vegetables in different ways.

Ribbons and shavings

The humble vegetable peeler can help to give fantastic texture to your salads. Simply running a veg peeler down the length of a carrot or courgette transforms the dense raw veg into soft ribbons or wisps, which absorb dressings, spices and pickle brines – giving you a mound of veg that's incredibly inviting and easy to eat.

You can also create ribbons of lettuce, cabbage and other leaves, like chard or kale, by thinly slicing them. These are equally moreish as they lap up dressings.

Other veg that respond well to the veg peeler shaving treatment include asparagus, beetroot, celeriac, cucumber, fennel, kohlrabi and parsnips.

I've included a couple of vegetable ribbon recipes in this book: Courgettes, toasted buckwheat, goat's cheese and dill (page 116) and Quick pickles (page 231), but do venture further with this technique, using it for other salads in the book, or as a canvas for your own creations.

Grated veg

An equally modest kitchen gadget is a standard box grater. As with a veg peeler, the box grater can alter the texture and eating experience of a variety of veg. Take parsnip, for instance. It's not a vegetable many would consider eating raw, but grated into snowy wisps, it's not only easier to munch your way through, but also incredibly accommodating when it comes to absorbing dressings and other flavours.

The acidity present in most dressings also helps soften grated veg, making it easier to eat and more digestible.

The following veg are particularly well suited to grating for salads: carrots, beetroot, courgettes, fennel, kohlrabi, parsnips, celeriac and turnips.

Grated veg shine in the recipes on pages 62, 198, 232 and 236, but again, do experiment further with this simple technique to add variety to the texture of your salads.

Diced veg

Dicing is the simplest way to cut up veg for salads, and you can make the pieces any size you like – from larger chunks of sweet crunchy apples or juicy tomatoes to toss though leaves, to finely diced fennel, celery and root veg to dress with a light vinaigrette or a richer mayo or yoghurt-based dressing. You can also add diced raw veg to cooked grains or pulses, to lend freshness and crunch, or roast the diced veg until softened into tempting nuggets, again to pair with grains, pulses or leaves.

Vegetable julienne and batons

Cutting veg into julienne involves slicing the veg into thin even-sized matchsticks, 1–2mm thick and around 4–5cm long. Batons are thicker (around 5mm) and, arguably, a more laid-back approach to sticks of veg, which offer texture but are also fine enough to absorb dressings and easy to eat.

The baton technique is best applied to root veg but you can also employ it for orchard fruits – apples, pears, and even quince. A hint of autumnal fruit, in the form of batons, will add a subtle hint of freshness and sweetness to Curried roots, pearl barley and parsley (page 77), for example.

You can also swap out some of the root veg in other salad recipes, and replace with rooty or fruity batons. Try using batons of carrot and beetroot in place of grated parsnips in the recipe on page 62, for a very different, yet equally tempting salad. Roast cauliflower with pumpkin seed satay (page 137) is really delicious, but it also works well with batons of carrot and parsnip in place of the cauli. Again, feel free to experiment and vary the recipes as you please.

1
QUICK

I was determined to open this book with the easiest recipes possible. I want to showcase salads as the simplest and speediest dishes you can create. You don't need an endless list of ingredients to make something that satisfies on every level. The recipes that follow take minutes to assemble and are composed of a handful of seasonal gems.

Amazing flavour always begins with great seasonal produce, followed by a good balance of tastes (a hint of sweetness, a pinch of salt, a lift of acidity), and great textures and colour. You can master this with as few as three ingredients: ripe, sun-kissed summer tomatoes straight from the vine with a pinch of local sea salt and a drizzle of good-quality olive oil. This trio has got to be one of the best combinations ever. To provide fresh inspiration, I've taken such classics and reinvigorated them with a nimble twist. For instance, adding raspberries and mint to tomatoes (see page 51), or coupling sauerkraut with red cabbage and apples (see page 46) for a zingy contrast that plays the role of salad dressing, too. Here, you don't even need to get a jam jar or whisk out to shake up a dressing.

There is a great synergy between the garden and the kitchen. It's often said: 'What grows together, goes together,' and you'll see and taste plenty of River Cottage kitchen garden-inspired matchmaking in this chapter. Many of the recipe ideas were hatched during a swift dash to the garden for a bundle of herbs, or by two ingredients simply being on the kitchen bench next to each other! Tasting one after the other, unintentionally, often leads to those culinary eureka moments, like when I realised how deliciously tomatoes pair with raspberries, melon with kohlrabi, or blushing dessert gooseberries with cucumber.

Fruit features significantly through this chapter because it plays so many roles. Notably, it works as a brilliant 'all-in-one' salad dressing that helps to harmonise mingling ingredients. Fruit is nature's perfect parcel of sweet and sour – two characteristics that lift a recipe. And, of course, the simple addition of fruit creates a wow factor both visually and on the palate.

Another secret to rustling up a quick salad is a simple squeeze of lemon, a sprinkling of seeds or a smattering of herbs. These can all completely transform a salad, turning a humble convergence of veg into a decidedly delicious meal. Such accessories can also unite rather unusual pairings, such as celeriac and rhubarb. Adding hazelnuts, parsley and lemon to a salad is like a sprinkling of magic dust that makes the dish sparkle, drawing you to dive in.

Sharp, tangy, umami-laden ingredients are also brilliantly transformative. Adding capers or kimchi alone to the most modest leaves delivers instant excitement. Invite a few other guests and you've got a party. My cucumber, grape, apple and almond combo with capers on page 52 certainly livens up a bowl of summer leaves.

The key to quick salads is knowing how to balance flavours, and that's really easy. Choosing ripe, juicy produce and enhancing it with something a little sour will set you up for delightful salad-making throughout the seasons. Use the recipes that follow as a guide, but experiment further – try new combinations, or mix and match some of my pairings for fresh creations of your own.

Red cabbage, apple, sauerkraut and parsley

A fresh autumnal salad that's easy to knock together when you're short on time. Red cabbages and apples are at their best at the same time of year and the sweet-sharpness of juicy crisp apple works so well with the slightly bitter raw cabbage and tangy sauerkraut.

Serves 2 as a light lunch, 4 as a side

1 small or ½ large red cabbage
A small bunch of flat-leaf parsley
150g good-quality sauerkraut
2 crisp eating apples, such as
  Gala or Cox
Sea salt and black pepper

Cut the cabbage into quarters, then remove and discard the tough core. Slice the cabbage finely and place in a large bowl. Pick the leaves from the parsley stalks and add them to the cabbage along with the sauerkraut. Season with salt and pepper, bearing in mind the sauerkraut lends a salty flavour.

Massage the ingredients together firmly with both hands for about a minute until the cabbage starts to soften and wilt slightly.

Quarter and core the apples, then cut into 2cm cubes. Toss the apple cubes through the cabbage. Taste and adjust the seasoning then serve straight away.

Swaps
For a spicier version, replace the apples with segmented oranges and the kraut with Kimkraut (see page 232).

Celeriac, rhubarb, hazelnuts and parsley

Celeriac is such a versatile veg – it's great roasted or mashed, but my favourite way to eat it is raw. It has a lovely crunchy texture and a slightly less intense flavour than its more commonly eaten relative, celery. Rhubarb, one of River Cottage's most-used ingredients, cuts through celeriac's almost creamy quality. Once you've tasted this I defy you not to make it a go-to salad.

Serves 2 as a main, 4 as a side

100g hazelnuts (skin on)
1 medium or ½ large celeriac (about 500g)
Juice of 2 lemons
2 sticks of rhubarb (about 150g)
A small bunch of flat-leaf parsley
Sea salt and black pepper

Preheat the oven to 200°C/Fan 180°C/Gas 6. Scatter the hazelnuts on a small baking tray and place in the oven for 8–10 minutes until the skins start to flake off. Remove from the oven, tip the nuts onto a cloth, fold it over and rub vigorously to encourage the skins to peel away. Transfer the nuts to a board, leaving the skin behind. Leave to cool.

Peel the celeriac and cut in half. Place both halves flat side down on a board and cut into 5mm thick slices, then cut across the slices to make 5mm batons. Place in a large bowl. Add the lemon juice and toss well.

Slice each stick of rhubarb lengthways into 4 or 5 strips and then cut across the strips to get nice even dice. Add to the celeriac.

Lightly crush the hazelnuts under the flat of a large kitchen knife or give them a quick bash using a pestle and mortar to just break them apart.

Pick the leaves from the parsley stalks and roughly chop them. Add to the salad with the toasted hazelnuts.

Tumble all the ingredients together to combine and season with salt and pepper to taste. Leave to stand for a few minutes before serving.

Swaps
Try swapping part or all of the celeriac out for thin batons of fennel or kohlrabi.

Tomatoes and raspberries with mint

I love adding fruit to dishes we consider to be savoury, as it takes them in a surprising direction. When I'm in the kitchen at River Cottage I taste everything, which often means I eat food in quick succession and in an odd order. Once, I'd just tried a simple tomato salad and then pinched a raspberry off the pastry section. I loved how they tasted together. Now I look forward to summer so I can put this back on the menu.

Serves 2 as a light lunch, 4 as a side

500g mixed heritage tomatoes
100g raspberries
3 sprigs of mint
2 tbsp extra virgin olive oil
Flaky sea salt and black pepper

Cut the tomatoes across into 5mm slices and arrange them over a large serving plate. Scatter the raspberries over the tomatoes.

Pick the leaves from the mint stalks, roughly tear them and sprinkle over the salad. Season with flaky salt and black pepper, then trickle over the olive oil. Enjoy!

Swaps
Use blackcurrants instead of raspberries for a sharper version, or towards the end of the summer add blackberries in place of some or all of the raspberries.

Cucumber, grapes, apple and almonds

This is a great example of simple ingredients paired well. Once assembled, the flavours and textures complement each other perfectly: sweet, juicy grapes balanced by salty capers, the fresh crunch of apple and cucumber contrasting with toasted, creamy almonds. It's a super-quick salad to put together, making it perfect for a light lunch.

Serves 2 as a light lunch, 4 as a side

50g almonds (skin on)
1 cucumber
200g green grapes
1 tbsp capers, drained, rinsed
   and roughly chopped
1 crisp eating apple, such as Cox
   or Gala
A large handful of soft lettuce
   leaves, such as Oakleaf or
   Lollo Rosso
Sea salt and black pepper

Place a small dry frying pan over a medium heat and add the almonds. Stir them over the heat for 3–4 minutes until they start to take on some colour and release their nutty aroma. Tip the almonds onto a board and leave to cool.

Quarter the cucumber lengthways then cut into 1cm dice and place in a large bowl.

Halve the grapes lengthways and remove any pips, then add to the cucumber with the capers. Quarter, core and thinly slice the apple and add to the salad.

Gently mix the ingredients together, season with salt and pepper to taste and allow the salad to sit for a couple of minutes. Meanwhile, roughly chop the toasted almonds.

After a few minutes the salad will have released a nice amount of juice. Toss the lettuce leaves through, then spread out the salad on a large serving plate and scatter over the almonds.

Swaps
When gooseberries are in season during the summer, use a handful instead of some of the grapes (as pictured); later in the year chicory works well in place of lettuce.

Seedy kale and kimchi with orange and seaweed dressing

We love fermenting at River Cottage and invariably have something resembling kimchi on the go. Adding the seaweed to this salad really boosts the umami flavour. You can turn this dish around in a matter of minutes and with so much flavour going on it is instantly satisfying.

Serves 2 as a main, 4 as a side

30g pumpkin seeds
30g sunflower seeds
400g curly kale or cavolo nero, thick stalks removed
100g kimchi or Kimkraut (see page 232)
Salt

For the dressing
1 orange
50g kimchi or Kimkraut (see page 232)
10g organic mixed seaweed flakes
2 tbsp cold-pressed rapeseed oil
1 tbsp tamari (or soy sauce)

Place a small dry frying pan over a medium heat and add the pumpkin and sunflower seeds. Heat, stirring occasionally, for a few minutes until the seeds start to colour. Tip them onto a plate and leave to cool.

Next make the dressing. Cut a thin slice from the top and bottom of the orange then stand it on a board and slice off the skin and white pith. Put the orange flesh into a jug blender and add the kimchi or Kimkraut, seaweed flakes, rapeseed oil and tamari or soy. Blend until smooth.

Bring a large pan of water to the boil over a high heat and add a little salt. Now add the kale and cook for 2 minutes until it is just wilted. Drain thoroughly in a colander, tossing to release all of the water.

Transfer the warm kale to a large bowl and add the kimchi or Kimkraut, dressing and toasted seeds. Toss together and serve straight away.

Swaps
Roasted wedges of hispi (pointed) cabbage, in place of the kale, work a treat. Cut the cabbage into thick wedges, toss in a little olive oil, season and place in a roasting tray. Roast in a preheated oven at 220°C/Fan 200°C/Gas 7 for 15–20 minutes.

Blackberries, pear, apple and oats

A perfect late summer treat, I love this – either for breakfast or as an early lunch on the go. It's also a favourite snack in our busy kitchen, fuelling us nicely through the day. The fruity combination hits the spot every time.

Serves 2 for breakfast, or lunch

40g rolled oats
40g pumpkin seeds
25g buckwheat groats
2 firm, ripe pears
1 crisp eating apple, such as Gala or Cox
25–30 ripe blackberries
3 tbsp organic natural yoghurt or kefir (optional)

Preheat the oven to 200°C/Fan 180°C/Gas 6. Scatter the oats, pumpkin seeds and buckwheat groats on a baking tray and place in the oven for 5 minutes. Give the tray a shake and a stir and return to the oven for a further 3–5 minutes until the mix is lightly toasted. Tip onto a plate and leave to cool.

Halve, peel and core the pears, then cut into slim wedges and place in a large bowl. Quarter and core the apple then cut into similar-sized wedges to the pears; add to the bowl.

Squish about half of the blackberries over the apples and pears and toss to mix. Add half of the toasted oat and seed mix, toss again and divide between individual bowls.

Scatter over the remaining blackberries and the rest of the toasted seed and oat mix. Serve with a dollop of yoghurt or kefir, if you like.

Swaps
The berries in this can change with the seasons, so start the summer with strawberries, then switch to blueberries, then raspberries and finally autumnal blackberries... they are all so delicious.

Cucumber, gooseberries, grapes and mint

This super-juicy salad uses mint to balance any undue sweetness from the fruit. Gooseberries are a much-loved ingredient here at River Cottage, especially the blushed dessert variety, which is only in season for a short time in the summer. When gooseberries are not available, use extra grapes. In the unlikely event you have any of this delicious salad left over, you can blitz it into an amazing gazpacho!

Serves 4 as a side

150g gooseberries, topped
  and tailed
75g green grapes
75g red grapes
1 cucumber
3 sprigs of mint
1 tbsp cold-pressed rapeseed oil
Sea salt and black pepper

Slice the gooseberries and grapes in half and remove any pips from the grapes. Quarter the cucumber lengthways then slice across into chunky pieces. Combine the gooseberries, grapes and cucumber in a large bowl.

Pick the mint leaves from their stalks and roughly tear them, then add to the salad. Trickle over the rapeseed oil and toss all the ingredients together. Season with a little salt and pepper to taste then serve.

Swaps
For a really crunchy version, try swapping the cucumber with sliced celery.

Parsnip, chicory, orange and prunes

You may have never eaten raw parsnip before but it's well worth a try. I wouldn't recommend munching on a big chunk as the texture and pepperiness would probably put you off, but by grating the parsnip you mellow it a great deal. The hit of natural fruit sugars from the prunes works perfectly with this earthy root.

Serves 4 as a side, 2 as a light lunch

2 small parsnips (the smaller and younger the better)
1 orange
1 white chicory bulb, finely sliced
100g prunes, torn into rough chunks
2 tbsp cold-pressed rapeseed oil
Sea salt and black pepper

Peel and grate the parsnips and place in a large bowl.

Cut a thin slice from the top and bottom of the orange then slice off the skin and white pith. Do this over the bowl of grated parsnip, so the segments and juice fall into the bowl.

Add the sliced chicory, prunes and rapeseed oil. Toss everything together and season with a little salt and pepper then serve.

Swaps
Try replacing the prunes with dates. During their short season, redcurrants work fantastically as an addition or as a swap for the prunes.

Tomatoes, Little Gem, capers and anchovies

We are a nation of tomato lovers and through the summer we grow some of the best tomatoes in the world. Heritage tomatoes – the funky-coloured ones – have become much more widely available and they offer not only colour but a great range of textures and flavours. Not to worry if you can't get hold of any; vine-ripened tomatoes will do the job nicely.

Serves 2 as a main, 4 as a side

600g mixed heritage tomatoes
1 tbsp capers, drained, rinsed and
　finely chopped
12 tinned or jarred anchovy fillets
　(MSC certified)
2 tbsp extra virgin olive oil
1 Little Gem lettuce, divided
　into leaves
Freshly cracked black pepper

Chop the tomatoes into 2cm pieces and place in a large bowl with the capers. Chop half of the anchovy fillets and add them to the bowl.

Trickle over the olive oil and gently toss through the tomatoes. Season with a little pepper (you won't need salt – the anchovies and capers add enough).

Carefully fold the lettuce leaves through the salad and top with the remaining whole anchovy fillets. Serve straight away.

Note If you have any of this salad left over, heat it gently in a pan until the tomatoes soften completely and then blitz into a delicious, smooth soup.

Swaps
In place of the anchovy fillets, you can use tinned MSC-certified sardines.

Peppery leaves with kohlrabi and melon

This often appears on the lunch table during a hectic day at River Cottage. A salad that has maximum impact with minimal input, it's an excellent side to serve alongside a barbecue, too. I love melon and all the other ingredients here just enhance it further.

Serves 2 as a light lunch, 4 as a side

1 medium kohlrabi
15g rocket
15g watercress, tougher stalks
    removed
15g pea shoots
Juice of 1 orange
1 tbsp cold-pressed rapeseed oil
¼ Cantaloupe melon
Sea salt and black pepper

Peel the kohlrabi and cut in half. Place both halves flat side down on a board and cut into 5mm slices, then cut across the slices to make 5mm thick batons. Place in a large bowl.

Add the rocket, watercress and pea shoots to the kohlrabi batons, season with a little salt and pepper and add the orange juice and rapeseed oil. Toss the salad to coat with the dressing.

Peel and deseed the melon, then cut lengthways into thin slices. Lay the melon slices over the base of a large shallow serving bowl and top with the kohlrabi and peppery leaf mix. Trickle over any juice left in the bowl. Serve straight away.

Swaps
Try using some blanched fresh peas instead of pea shoots, and fennel batons instead of kohlrabi.

Leftover roast beef with rocket and horseradish crème fraîche

We're all guilty of cooking too much sometimes. Using those leftovers is not only seriously important but they should be seriously tasty. Hot horseradish and peppery rocket are brilliant with beef here, but they go with any red meat. I recommend you serve this with some crusty bread on the side but you'll also catch me loading it into two slices of bread – with heaps of the horseradish crème fraîche – for a proper doorstep sarnie.

Serves 2–3 as a lunch

25g fresh horseradish, or
    50g good-quality fiery
    horseradish sauce
200g full-fat crème fraîche
1 tsp Dijon mustard
About 6 generous slices of leftover
    roast beef (or any other cooked
    red meat)
50g rocket
2 tbsp cold-pressed rapeseed oil
1 small red onion, finely sliced
    into rings
Sea salt and black pepper

If you're using fresh horseradish, peel then grate it on the finest grater you have – this will release a hot pungent aroma so don't breathe too deeply!

Mix the grated horseradish, or the horseradish sauce if using, into the crème fraîche with the Dijon mustard, and season with a little salt and black pepper.

Lay the slices of roast beef on a serving plate and allow them to come to room temperature. Generously dollop the horseradish crème fraîche onto the plate.

Toss the rocket with the rapeseed oil and pile onto the plate. Finish with the red onion slices and season with salt and pepper. Serve with crusty sourdough.

Note If you have any horseradish crème fraîche left, save it to pep up a roast beef sandwich or smoked mackerel.

Swaps
Switch out the rocket for any peppery leaf: watercress, mizuna and mustard greens all work well.

2
HEARTY

Big, colourful and comforting salads that can feature as the main event or the centrepiece of any meal is what this chapter is all about. (Side is a moniker attached to salads far too often and I'm determined to change that.) The vibrancy and variety a brilliant, well-constructed salad can bring to the table, paired with its robust ability to satisfy your appetite and nourish your body, more than justifies a prominent space on the table for these dishes.

The warm, generous recipes that follow will fortify you for long country walks or welcome you in after a chilly day spent outside. Curried roots, pearled barley and parsley (page 77) is one of my all-time favourite post- (or pre-) Bonfire Night dishes – it's the perfect hearty dish to share. Sticky beef, bean sprouts and coriander (page 99) works pretty much all year round and is as wonderful on a hazy summer evening outside as it is on a wintry day. Kale, apple, goat's cheese and hazelnut butter (page 74) is a salad I always crave and often take as a filling companion on a brisk autumnal hike in the woods.

Food is so emotive and can give us so much pleasure. A salad might not be the first thing that springs to mind when you think of comfort food, but I think the dishes I've packed into this chapter fit the bill. Kidney beans with smoky tomato and onion salsa (page 86) is a great favourite with my family and has become our go-to movie-night meal – a healthy, yet hearty, swap for pizza. It's versatile, too. While it can certainly stand on its own, we often have it wrapped into fajitas or spooned over a cheesy jacket potato. A deeply satisfying dish can shape special moments and make them more memorable.

I've also nestled some great techniques into this chapter, most notably char-grilling. I think you'll love it and hopefully use it loads! The intense application of heat really transforms veg and fruit. You get such rich, umami flavours, exciting textures and, visually, all the caramelised edges on things like clementines, leeks or cabbage look so inviting.

I've also bundled an easy but truly delicious homemade curd cheese recipe into the charred courgettes, broad beans and mangetout recipe on page 88. Make extra curds and you can add them to so many other dishes – they are exceptionally good alongside flame-roasted summer or early autumn veg. Another gem which you can intermingle with so many other dishes is my pickled pears on page 83. In the winter you can tuck them into the Cavolo, peach, cashews and blue cheese salad on page 97 in place of the summer peaches.

What makes a salad hearty is a playful mix of substantial ingredients. All the recipes that follow are bolstered with nourishing grains, toasted nuts and seeds, moreish sprinklings of cheese and the sharp addictive tang of homemade pickles. There are lots of enticing ways of preparing simple ingredients to make them really stand out and lure you to get stuck in. I hope some of the salads in this chapter will become firm favourites with your family. Perhaps they'll even stir playful bunfight moments as you all wrestle over who gets the last bite.

Kale, apple, goat's cheese and hazelnut butter

This was first made for a big garden open day we had at River Cottage and it was a winner. We happened to have a massive harvest of mixed kale from the garden and apples from the orchard, and dressing the kale with the hazelnut butter worked a treat. The way the hazelnut butter clings to the leaves makes it so moreish. A great autumn dish – wonderfully satisfying after a long walk.

Serves 2 as a main

300g cavolo nero or curly kale
   (or a mix), thick stalks removed
1 crisp eating apple, such as Gala
   or Cox
2 tbsp olive oil
2 garlic cloves, sliced
50g hazelnuts, roughly chopped
100ml dry cider
2 tbsp hazelnut butter, ideally
   crunchy, but smooth will do
   (or you could use peanut butter)
150g soft goat's cheese
Sea salt and black pepper

Roughly chop the cavolo or kale. Quarter, core and slice the apple.

Place a large saucepan or wok over a medium heat and add the olive oil. Toss in the garlic and chopped hazelnuts and cook for a minute, stirring constantly.

Increase the heat to high and add the apple and cavolo or kale to the pan. Toss to mix, add the cider and cook, stirring often, until the kale starts to wilt down.

If the hazelnut butter is a bit thick, mix it with a little extra cider or a splash of water to loosen it.

Add the hazelnut butter to the pan and mix through well. Season with salt and pepper to taste. Break the goat's cheese into small pieces and scatter over the warm salad. Serve at once.

Swaps
Any greens will do here, even shredded cabbage; roasted cauliflower florets are also a great swap.

Curried roots, pearled barley and parsley

Root vegetables love curry spices and this warming dish is ideal for a chilly autumn evening. At River Cottage, it normally makes an appearance on Bonfire Night served hot, but it's equally delicious warm or served at room temperature. Any leftovers can be topped with some grated cheese and baked for a quick lunch the next day.

Serves 4 as a main, 6–8 as a side

100g pearled barley or spelt,
   ideally pre-soaked (for at least
   20 minutes, preferably overnight)
250g parsnips
250g carrots
250g celeriac
20g good-quality medium-hot
   curry powder
1 tsp fennel seeds
1 tsp nigella seeds
2 tbsp sunflower oil
50g flat-leaf parsley
Sea salt and black pepper

Put the pearled barley or spelt into a saucepan, cover with water and bring to the boil over a high heat. Lower the heat and simmer until just softened but retaining a little bite: 30–35 minutes for barley; 15–20 minutes for spelt. Remove from the heat and drain in a sieve then rinse under cold running water to remove any excess starch. Leave to cool.

Preheat the oven to 210°C/Fan 190°C/Gas 6½. Peel and halve or quarter the parsnips and carrots, depending on size. Peel the celeriac and cut in half then place both halves flat side down on a board and cut into 1.5cm thick slices. Cut across the slices to make batons.

Place all the prepared root veg in a large bowl. Add the curry powder, fennel and nigella seeds, and the sunflower oil. Toss together and season with salt and pepper.

Spread the veg out in a single layer in a large roasting dish and roast for 10 minutes. Give the veg a stir around and return to the oven for 10–15 minutes until golden brown and just starting to soften.

Add the barley or spelt to the roasting dish and mix with the roots. Place back in the oven for a further 5 minutes. Pick the leaves from the parsley stalks and scatter over the roasted veg and grains before serving.

Swaps
Swap out one of the roots for a nice fluffy potato like Maris Piper.

Swede, sprouts, chestnuts and char-grilled clementines

Everyone has an opinion on sprouts; it's the ultimate Marmite vegetable. If you love them, this warm salad is a gem, but if you're not a fan I still urge you to give it a try – it could change your view. It's an ideal salad for a lighter meal around Christmas, when you're almost certain to have all of the ingredients in the house. Once charred, the clementines become soft and sweeter – no need to peel, you can eat them whole, skin and all!

Serves 4 as a main, 6–8 as a starter

1 medium swede
2 tbsp cold-pressed rapeseed oil
500g Brussels sprouts, halved
200g peeled cooked chestnuts,
    broken into pieces
1 tbsp sumac
100g prunes, halved
5 clementines, halved crossways
1 red chicory bulb, divided into
    leaves
A bunch of flat-leaf parsley (30g),
    leaves picked
Sea salt and black pepper

Preheat the oven to 220°C/Fan 200°C/Gas 7. Peel the swede, cut into 2cm cubes and tip into a bowl. Trickle over the rapeseed oil, season with salt and pepper and toss to coat. Tip the swede into a roasting tray, spread out in a single layer and roast in the oven for 15 minutes.

Take the tray from the oven and add the Brussels sprouts, chestnuts, sumac and prunes. Toss through the swede, then return to the oven for a further 15 minutes until the swede is just softened.

About 10 minutes before the veg will be ready, heat up a cast-iron griddle pan over a high heat until smoking hot. Place the clementines flesh side down in the pan and cook for about 3–4 minutes without moving until you get a good char. Turn the clementines over and cook on the skin side for 2–3 minutes. You should be able to see the juices start to bubble up through the cut surface.

Toss the chicory and parsley leaves through the roasted veg and taste to check the seasoning. Just before serving, squeeze a couple of clementine halves over the veg to release their juice as a dressing.

Serve the warm salad with the remaining char-grilled clementine halves on the side.

Swaps
The swede is interchangeable with any root veg. Parsnips and celeriac are especially good.

Char-grilled cabbage, pickled pears, pesto and walnuts

Charring cabbage works beautifully and the smoky flavour it takes on makes it deeply satisfying and filling. Pickled pears, toasted walnuts and a pumpkin seed and basil pesto enhance it to delicious effect in this warming salad. Once the dish is on the table it won't last long. If you can't get hold of a hispi, you can use any other firm, compact cabbage.

Both the pears and pesto will keep in the fridge for up to a week so I often make more than I need. The pickled pears are the ideal partner to some late-night cheese; the pesto is perfect with pasta.

Serves 2 as a main, 4 as a side

For the pickled pears
1 tsp cumin seeds
1 tsp coriander seeds
200ml cider vinegar
200ml water
½ tsp dried chilli flakes
½ tsp salt
2 large firm, ripe pears

For the pesto
75g pumpkin seeds
2 bunches of basil (about 150g in total), leaves picked
1 large or 2 small garlic cloves, roughly chopped
200ml extra virgin olive oil
Juice of 1 lemon
Sea salt and black pepper

To assemble
2 small hispi (or pointed) cabbages
100g walnuts

To prepare the pickled pears, place a medium saucepan over a medium heat and add the cumin and coriander seeds. Toast until they take on a little colour and start to release their aroma. Add the cider vinegar, water, chilli flakes and salt, turn the heat right down and slowly bring to a low simmer to allow the seeds to infuse their flavour.

Meanwhile, peel, quarter and core the pears. Cut each quarter into 4 or 5 thin wedges and place in a heatproof bowl. Pour the hot pickling liquor over the pears and cover with a small plate that fits inside the bowl to weigh them down and keep them submerged. Leave to cool. (At this stage they can be kept in the fridge for up to a week.)

To make the pesto, place a medium frying pan over a medium heat and add the pumpkin seeds. Heat, stirring occasionally, until they start to colour and release their aroma. Tip onto a plate and leave to cool.

Put the basil, garlic, pumpkin seeds and olive oil into a small blender and pulse to a rough paste. Season with salt and pepper and set aside. (The lemon juice is added at the last minute; if added now it will discolour the pesto.)

If you're cooking outside, heat up the barbecue and let the fire die down a bit, but you need a pretty intense heat.

If you're cooking indoors, heat a cast-iron griddle pan over a medium-high heat on the hob until smoking hot.

Cut the cabbages into quarters. Once the barbecue is ready or the griddle pan is hot, add the cabbage wedges and cook until charred on all sides. Move the wedges to the cooler edge of the barbecue or lower the heat under the griddle and cook for a little longer until the thicker leaf bases start to become tender (the fibrous stem base won't cook through, but that will be removed).

Place a small dry frying pan over a medium heat, add the walnuts and toast for a few minutes until they start to release their aroma. Take off the heat.

Lay the charred cabbage wedges on a board and remove the hard stem base; this will allow the leaves to separate. Season with salt and pepper and spread out on a large serving platter.

Stir the lemon juice through the pesto. Drain the pears, saving a few spoonfuls of the liquor, and distribute them over the cabbage. Trickle over the saved liquor and dollop the pesto on top of the cabbage and pears. Scatter the walnuts over the warm salad and serve.

Swaps
Through late spring and early summer, grill tight-headed lettuce such as Little Gem instead of the cabbage. They will only need about a minute on each side.

Kidney beans with smoky tomato and onion salsa

The salsa in this dish is a winner: fresh, hot and smoky. Once you've tasted it you'll find an excuse to make it for other meals. It's best with beans but it's also great piled into tacos, wrapped in tortillas with veg or chicken to eat as fajitas, or spooned all over a cheesy jacket potato. It's also good with grilled fish and roasted veg. Tossed through kidney beans, as here, it really brings them to life for a satisfying spicy supper.

Serves 2 as a main, 4 as a side

For the salsa

1 tsp cumin seeds
4 ripe medium tomatoes
 (about 200g)
1 small red onion
1 garlic clove, finely chopped or
 grated
1 tsp dried chipotle chilli flakes,
 or to taste
Juice of 1 lime
2 tbsp extra virgin olive oil
Sea salt and black pepper

To assemble

400g tin kidney beans, drained
 and rinsed
A bunch of coriander (50g)

First make the salsa. Place a small dry frying pan over a medium heat and add the cumin seeds. Heat, stirring occasionally, until they start to colour and release their aroma. Tip them onto a plate and leave to cool completely, then grind to a fine powder.

Finely chop the tomatoes and red onion into 5mm dice and tip into a large bowl. Add the garlic, chilli flakes (adding another pinch of these if you like it hot) and the ground cumin seeds. Trickle over the lime juice and olive oil, season with salt and pepper and mix well. Leave to stand for an hour to allow the flavours to mingle.

Once the salsa is ready, mix it through the beans. Pick the leaves from the coriander stalks and scatter them over the salad before serving. Any leftovers will keep in the fridge for a couple of days.

Note You can also serve this hot. Just heat up the kidney beans in a saucepan, stirring carefully so as not to break them up, then toss through the salsa.

Swaps
A mix of freshly podded broad beans and peas is a lovely summery alternative to the kidney beans.

Charred courgettes, broad beans, mangetout and fresh curds

Courgettes are easy to grow if you have a bit of space and their yield is usually impressive, so I'm always looking for different ways to treat them. Grilling them over fire is my absolute favourite – it concentrates the flavours and lends a lovely smoky taste. The curds are firm – like an instant fresh cheese – and make a great addition to almost any salad.

Serves 2 as a main, 4 as a side

For the curds
1 litre milk
Juice of 1 lemon
2 tbsp extra virgin olive oil
Sea salt and black pepper

For the veg
150g podded broad beans
150g peas (freshly picked and podded or frozen)
75g mangetout, halved
3 courgettes
½ small radicchio, divided into leaves
A small bunch of flat-leaf parsley, leaves picked
Juice of 1 orange
2 tbsp extra virgin olive oil

To make the curds, bring the milk to a simmer in a large saucepan over a medium-low heat, then add the lemon juice and stir until the milk splits into curds. Tip into a fine sieve to drain off the liquid, then transfer to a bowl. While still warm, dress the curds with the olive oil and season with salt and pepper. They will keep in a sealed container in the fridge for 3 days.

If you're cooking outside, heat up the barbecue and allow the fire to die down until the coals are glowing red.

Meanwhile, bring a large pan of water to the boil over a high heat and add a little salt. Add the broad beans, followed 30 seconds later by the peas, then after a further 30 seconds add the mangetout. Cook for a further 30 seconds and then tip into a colander to drain. Allow to cool then transfer to a large bowl.

If you're cooking indoors, heat a cast-iron griddle pan over a medium-high heat on the hob until smoking hot.

Slice the courgettes on the diagonal into 1cm thick slices. Once the fire is ready or the griddle pan is hot, add the courgette slices and cook, turning once, until charred on both sides. (If using a griddle pan you may need to do this in batches.)

Add the charred courgettes to the peas and beans with the radicchio and parsley. Add the orange juice and olive oil, season with salt and pepper to taste and toss to mix. Transfer the salad to a warmed platter, scatter over the curds and serve.

Barbecued leeks, spelt and sunflower seeds

I like to cook leeks over fire as it gives them a deep smoky flavour; they also develop a lot of sweetness as they cook. If you're a fan of smoky flavours, include the charred outside of the leek; if you prefer a mellower taste, discard it.

Serves 4 as a main, 6–8 as a side

200g pearled spelt or barley, ideally pre-soaked (for at least 20 minutes, preferably overnight)
3 medium leeks, dark green tops removed
60g sunflower seeds
2 garlic cloves, finely chopped or grated
A bunch of chives (30g), finely chopped
Juice of 2 lemons
3 tbsp cold-pressed rapeseed oil
Sea salt and black pepper

Put the pearled spelt or barley into a saucepan, cover with water and bring to the boil over a high heat. Lower the heat and simmer until just softened but retaining a little bite: 15–20 minutes for spelt; 30–35 minutes for barley. Remove from the heat and drain in a sieve then rinse under cold running water to remove any excess starch. Leave to cool.

If you are cooking outside, heat up the barbecue and allow the fire to die down a bit, but you need a good fierce heat.

If you're cooking indoors, heat a cast-iron griddle pan over a medium-high heat on the hob until smoking hot.

Halve the leeks lengthways and wash thoroughly. Once the barbecue is ready or the griddle pan is hot, add the halved leeks and cook, turning once, until each side is charred. Remove from the heat and leave until cool enough to handle, then cut into thin slices.

Place a small dry frying pan over a medium heat and add the sunflower seeds. Heat, stirring occasionally, until they start to colour and release their aroma. Take off the heat.

Put the spelt, leeks and sunflower seeds into a large bowl and add the garlic, chives, lemon juice and rapeseed oil. Toss everything together and season with salt and pepper to taste. Serve straight away.

Swaps
Try using brown rice or farro instead of spelt or barley, adjusting the cooking time accordingly.

Beetroot three ways with tamari seeds

Beetroot is such a versatile ingredient yet it is so often underestimated. Available all year round, it is at its best from May to late September. By treating it in three contrasting ways – pickled, roasted and raw – you really get the best out of it. Here I've used different varieties, including the candy-striped Chioggia, but use whatever you can get hold of. Look for beetroot with some stalk still attached – a good indication of freshness.

Serves 2 as a main

For the pickled beetroot
1 golf-ball-sized beetroot, ideally
   Chioggia
200ml cider vinegar
200ml water
1 tsp fennel seeds
1 tsp cumin seeds
1 tsp coriander seeds

For the tamari seeds
50g pumpkin seeds
50g sunflower seeds
2 tbsp tamari (or soy sauce)

For the roasted beetroot
5 red beetroot (golf-ball-sized)
4 golden beetroots (golf-ball-sized)
2–3 tbsp olive oil
Sea salt and black pepper

For the raw beetroot
1 golf-ball-sized beetroot, ideally
   candy-striped Chioggia
A little extra virgin olive oil

To assemble and serve
3–4 tbsp full-fat cottage cheese
A small bunch of dill, sprigs picked

To prepare the pickled beetroot, peel the beetroot and slice as finely as possible, preferably using a mandoline. Put into a heatproof bowl or jar and set aside.

Pour the cider vinegar and water into a saucepan and add the fennel, cumin and coriander seeds with a pinch of salt. Slowly bring to the boil over a low heat to infuse the liquid with the spice seeds, then remove from the heat and strain through a sieve into a jug to remove the seeds.

Pour the hot strained liquor over the sliced beetroot, making sure it is completely covered, and leave to cool to room temperature. (Any pickle that you won't use straight away can be kept in a clean, sterilised jar with a tight-fitting lid in the fridge for up to a month.)

For the tamari seeds, preheat the oven to 200°C/Fan 180°C/Gas 6. Toss the pumpkin and sunflower seeds with the tamari or soy on a baking tray and spread them out. Toast in the oven for 5 minutes, then give them a stir and return to the oven for a further 2 minutes. Remove from the oven and allow to cool.

For the roasted beetroot, place the red and golden varieties in separate roasting trays (to stop the red beetroot dyeing the golden ones a shade of pink). Pour a little water into each tray and cover with foil. Roast in the oven at 200°C/Fan 180°C/Gas 6 for 30–40 minutes or until the beetroot are just tender, shaking the trays halfway through cooking.

Remove the trays from the oven and leave until cool enough to handle, then peel off the skin (peel the golden beetroot first so you don't smudge them pink with the juices from the red ones).

Turn the oven up to 220°C/Fan 200°C/Gas 7. Cut the beetroot into quarters and return them to the roasting trays. Trickle over a little olive oil and season with salt and pepper. Roast in the oven for a further 15–20 minutes until the beetroot are caramelised at the edges.

While the beetroot are in the oven, peel the raw Chioggia beetroot and slice as thinly as you can, preferably using a mandoline. Place in a bowl, add a trickle of olive oil and season with salt and pepper. Toss lightly.

To assemble, drain your pickled beetroot and pat dry. Arrange the roasted, pickled and raw beetroot on a large serving platter, spoon on the cottage cheese and sprinkle with the tamari seeds. Tear the dill into smaller sprigs and scatter over the salad. Serve at once.

Swaps

Try using a fuller flavoured cheese. A crumbly blue works well, as does a strong mature Cheddar.

Cavolo, peach, cashews and blue cheese

This satisfying salad is perfect for a warm summer's evening. The deep, earthy flavour of cavolo nero is counteracted by the sweetness of the peach and the saltiness of the cheese. It's all cooked in one pan so you can prepare it with ease.

Serves 2 as a main

250g cavolo nero or curly kale
1 ripe peach
2 tbsp extra virgin olive oil
1 garlic clove, sliced
50g cashew nuts
150g Beenleigh Blue or other
    good crumbly blue cheese, or
    an ash-coated goat's cheese
Sea salt and black pepper

Remove the thick stalks from the cavolo or kale and roughly tear the leaves. Halve, stone and slice the peach.

Place a large saucepan over a medium heat and add the olive oil. When hot, add the garlic and cashew nuts and cook, stirring, until the garlic takes on a little colour.

Add the kale and peach slices to the pan and turn up the heat to high. Cook briefly, stirring constantly, until the kale starts to wilt down. Take off the heat and season with salt and pepper to taste.

Transfer the salad to a warmed platter, crumble over the cheese and serve.

Swaps
Substitute an apple or pear for the peach when the fruit isn't in season; both work well.

Sticky beef, bean sprouts and coriander

Full of amazing flavours and textures, this is so delicious, it's almost addictive! Make sure you get the scrapings off the tray you cook the beef on, as they're the best bits...

Serves 2 as a main

300g leftover roast beef, or 300g piece braising beef, such as neck
3 tbsp honey
3 tbsp tamari (or soy sauce)
10g coriander seeds
Juice of 2 limes
½ red chilli, deseeded and finely chopped
100g bean sprouts
1 carrot, cut into fine batons
1 small red onion, finely sliced
50g spring onions, finely sliced
¼ Savoy cabbage, cored and finely sliced
1 small courgette, finely diced
A small bunch of coriander (30g), leaves picked
Sea salt and black pepper

If using fresh beef, preheat the oven to 170°C/Fan 150°C/Gas 3. Place the beef in a roasting dish with a little water, cover with foil and cook for 2–3 hours or until the beef is soft and falling apart. Remove from the oven and allow to cool.

Tear the leftover or freshly cooked beef into rough strips and place in a bowl. Mix the honey, tamari, coriander seeds, lime juice and chilli together in a small bowl and then add to the beef and toss to combine.

Heat the oven to 190°C/Fan 170°C/Gas 5. Line a baking tray with greaseproof paper and spread the beef out in a single layer on the tray.

Pop the tray in the oven for 6 minutes. Take it out and turn the beef, mixing it through any sauce on the tray, then return to the oven for a further 6 minutes. Repeat this process 3 or 4 times until the beef is sticky.

Meanwhile, combine all the prepared veg in a bowl. Roughly chop the coriander and add to the veg. Season with salt and pepper to taste and mix together.

Just before serving, toss the warm beef through the veg and serve warm.

Swaps
Lamb, pork and duck are all good alternatives to the beef. It's a great dish to use up leftover meat.

3
LIGHT

This chapter hones in on the lighter end of the salad spectrum, admittedly with a sunny, summer bias. The warmer months offer abundance and a host of vibrant flavours. Juicy berries, succulent tomatoes, grassy asparagus, delicate nuggets of white crab meat, aromatic herbs, the sweet pop of garden peas, crisp Little Gems and peppery radishes, to name but a few. These flavour-rich gems need minimal accessorising to become enticing salads.

A mere squeeze of citrus is all you need to dress many of them, and they're easy to assemble, too. If you're looking for an accompaniment to a main meal, or a selection of small salads to balance richer dishes, you should find plenty of inspiration here. You might just want a healthy snack to tide you over until the next meal. If so, you'll find something tempting here that will provide nourishment but nothing heavy to weigh you down.

Most salads in this chapter are rich in raw ingredients, so they're pretty light on preparation, too. Peppery tangles of watercress pair with juice-bursting orange segments (see page 126); the apple-like crispness of kohlrabi harmonises with the sharp, tangy zing of blackcurrants (see page 121); and raw courgettes, which are so surprisingly refreshing, are enhanced with lemon and the soft aniseed whisper of dill (see page 116). The sweetness and subtle acidity of sun-drenched tomatoes tantalise the palate by themselves, but even more so when partnered with crisp cucumber, tart redcurrants, and tingling mint (see page 106).

I've also included a couple of delicious seafood recipes in this chapter, featuring crab and squid. Whenever you're looking to make a fish salad, seek local (if possible), seasonal and line-caught fish and look for the blue MSC eco-label 'tick' or consult the Marine Conservation Society's online Good Fish Guide to help guide you.

Herbs feature prominently in these salads, as they brighten any dish and are a brilliant way of adding complexity to a salad without weighing it down. Dip into my section on herbs (with advice on how to grow your own) on pages 33–6. While I've woven a fragrant abundance through the book, you can have fun swapping herbs in and out of salads, or by adding several varieties to a single dish. Palate-cleansing mint, dill and parsley feature strongly in the following recipes but lemon verbena, tarragon and any of the basil varieties – from deep purple to delicate Greek varieties – will enliven a salad too.

Ebbing into the cooler months, I've kept things light by adding autumnal and winter crunch. Apples, celery and fennel are bound together with a velvety dressing made with almonds that tickles the taste buds and is the antithesis of cloying (see page 114). Grilled pears are a luxurious, buttery, yet refreshing foil to the pretty bitter leaves of blushing chicory and gently toasted walnuts (see page 119). I also have a simple autumn/winter fruit offering of sharp apples with a tantalising twist of lime and a crumbling of warm, pan-roasted hazelnuts (on page 113), which makes a delicious snack at any time of the day.

All these wonderful light salads are not only the perfect way of embellishing your day with delightful flavours and nourishment, they also help you tread lightly when it comes to your carbon footprint. They're lush with fresh ingredients that sing with the seasons, requiring little input from you or the environment. They're dishes that dazzle in every possible way.

Roast asparagus, feta, almonds and sourdough croûtons

Asparagus is one of the first signs of spring: as the weather warms slightly the brilliant green spears start to poke through the earth. Typically, the short asparagus season ends around the summer solstice, so the last of the crop heralds the start of summer. For this salad the spears are roasted to enhance their amazing flavour, while retaining a good crunch.

Serves 2 as a main, 4 as a starter

2 slices slightly stale sourdough or
   good-quality wholemeal bread,
   crusts removed
3 tbsp extra virgin olive oil
100g almonds (skin on), roughly
   chopped
About 500g asparagus
   (at least 16 spears)
1 Little Gem lettuce, divided
   into leaves
150g good-quality feta
Juice of 1 lemon
Sea salt and black pepper

Preheat the oven to 230°C/Fan 210°C/Gas 8. Cut the bread into 1cm cubes and place in a bowl with 2 tbsp of the olive oil and some salt and pepper. Toss to coat.

Scatter the bread cubes on a baking tray and toast in the oven for 5 minutes until golden brown and crunchy. Tip the croûtons onto a plate and allow to cool.

Spread the chopped almonds out on the baking tray and toast in the oven for 3 minutes then set aside to cool.

Break off the tough ends of the asparagus and cut the spears in half on the diagonal. Place on a baking tray, trickle over the remaining 1 tbsp olive oil and season with salt and pepper. Roast the asparagus in the oven for 4 minutes, then remove and set aside for a few minutes to cool slightly.

Transfer the roasted asparagus to a large bowl and add the almonds, lettuce leaves and croûtons. Crumble in the feta cheese, then trickle over the lemon juice. Add a touch more seasoning if you feel it needs it, and serve.

Swaps
Once the asparagus season is over, grill plump spring onions instead.

Tomatoes, cucumber, redcurrants and mint

I think of this as summer in a bowl. For a few months our polytunnels are overflowing with tomatoes and cucumbers and the redcurrant bushes are in full fruit in the garden at the same time. Looking magical with their translucent scarlet skins, these fruits are almost ornamental in their beauty. Eat this salad outside in the sun and happiness will ensue!

Serves 2 as a main, 4 as a side

600g heritage tomatoes
1 cucumber
1 garlic clove, finely chopped
   or grated
2 sprigs of mint
2 tbsp extra virgin olive oil
100g redcurrants
Sea salt and black pepper

Chop the tomatoes and place in a large bowl. Quarter the cucumber lengthways then cut across into 1cm pieces and add to the tomatoes with the garlic.

Pick the leaves from the mint stalks, roughly tear them and sprinkle over the salad. Trickle over the olive oil, season with a little salt and pepper and gently tumble everything together.

Tip into a serving bowl, scatter over the redcurrants and serve straight away.

Swaps
For a fruitier version try replacing the cucumber with honeydew melon.

Peas, mint, Oakleaf lettuce and grapes

This delightful assembly is perfect for a quick lunch. The grapes and peas lend a mild sweetness, which is complemented by the bright, bold mint. It's a fabulous salad on its own but also particularly good with a soft, salty goat's cheese or some smoked mackerel.

Serves 2 as a main, 4 as a side

200g peas (freshly picked and
    podded or frozen)
A small bunch of green grapes
    (200g)
3 sprigs of mint
Juice of 1 lemon
1 tbsp extra virgin olive oil
1 small Oakleaf lettuce, divided
    into leaves

Bring a pan of water to the boil, add the peas and cook for 1 minute. Drain in a colander and allow to cool, tossing the peas occasionally to ensure they cool quite quickly.

Halve the grapes lengthways and remove any pips. Pick the leaves from the mint stalks and roughly chop them.

Put the peas, grapes and mint into a large bowl. Trickle over the lemon juice and olive oil and toss gently.

Just before serving, add the lettuce leaves and fold through the salad. Transfer to a serving platter and serve straight away, before the lettuce starts to wilt.

Swaps
When they are at their summery best, gooseberries are lovely in this salad instead of grapes.

Apple with toasted hazelnuts and lime

Limes bring apples to life. This is super simple but such a joy to eat – I'll often snack on a bowlful as I work. It works particularly well as a sharp, sweet salad on the side of a creamy dessert... a great all-rounder.

Serves 4 as a side

50g hazelnuts
2 crisp eating apples, such
   as Cox, Gala or Russet
Finely grated zest and juice
   of 2 limes

Lightly crush the hazelnuts under the flat of a large kitchen knife or give them a quick bash using a pestle and mortar to just break them apart.

Place a small frying pan over a medium heat, add the hazelnuts and heat, stirring occasionally, until they start to take on some colour and release their nutty aroma. Tip onto a plate and allow to cool.

Quarter, core and slice the apples. Place them in a bowl with the hazelnuts and add the lime zest and juice. Toss together and tuck in!

Swaps
For a sweeter salad, replace one of the apples with about 100g strawberries, halved.

Fennel, celery and apple with creamy almond dressing

This salad is all about the crisp crunch of the fennel and celery, and the way these big bold flavours are tamed by the creamy almond dressing. Delicious on its own, it's also a lovely accompaniment to grilled fish. The dressing goes with almost anything and keeps in the fridge for a week, so I often make a double batch. Try dunking lettuce leaves into it... delicious.

Serves 2 as a main, 4 as a side

50g almonds (skin on), roughly
   chopped
2 crisp eating apples, such as
   Gala or Cox
2 fennel bulbs
5 celery sticks
A handful of pea shoots
   (about 40g)

For the almond dressing
100g almonds (skin on)
150ml almond milk or water
1 orange
60ml extra virgin olive oil
30ml cider vinegar
1 small garlic clove, peeled
Sea salt and black pepper

First make the dressing, a day ahead if you can. Put the almonds into a bowl, pour on the almond milk or water, cover and leave to soak overnight. (Or put the almonds in a pan with the liquid, cover and place over a low heat for 15–20 minutes to slightly soften them, then leave to cool.)

Cut a thin slice from the top and bottom of the orange then stand it on a board and slice off the skin and white pith. Cut the orange segments out from between the membranes, remove any pips then place in a jug blender.

Add the olive oil, cider vinegar, garlic and softened almonds to the blender along with any remaining soaking liquor. Blitz to form a smooth dressing. If it's a little too thick, add almond milk or water 1 tbsp at a time, until the desired consistency is reached. Season with salt and pepper to taste. Set aside.

Place a small frying pan over a medium heat, add the chopped almonds and heat, stirring occasionally, until they start to take on some colour and release their nutty aroma. Tip onto a plate and allow to cool.

Quarter, core and dice the apples into very small cubes and place in a large bowl. Quarter the fennel bulbs, cut into 5mm thick slices and add to the bowl. Finely slice the celery into 5mm slices and add these too. Add half of the pea shoots to the salad, then trickle over the dressing and toss until all the veg are nicely coated.

Transfer the salad to a serving platter and scatter over the remaining pea shoots and toasted almonds to serve.

Courgettes, toasted buckwheat, goat's cheese and dill

If you've ever grown courgettes you know you never just grow one! Over the years we've created many a dish to get through the inevitable glut. Eating them raw is probably my favourite way to enjoy them, as they have a delicate apple-y flavour. As soon as the lemon juice hits them, though, they start to break down, so preparing everything for this dish in advance is key, then you can assemble it at the last minute.

Serves 2 as a main, 4 as a side

50g buckwheat groats
3 medium courgettes
Juice of 2 lemons
100g organic soft goat's cheese
A small bunch of dill (about 20g)
3 tbsp cold-pressed rapeseed oil
Sea salt and black pepper

Place a medium frying pan over a medium heat. Add the buckwheat groats and stir occasionally until they take on a little colour and you can smell the toasted buckwheat.

Using a swivel vegetable peeler, pare the courgettes along their length into long ribbons. Place them in a large bowl. (It will look like a lot of courgette ribbons at this stage.)

Just before serving, pour the lemon juice over the courgette ribbons and season with salt and pepper to taste. Toss gently and the courgettes will start to soften and reduce down. Transfer to a serving dish.

Break the goat's cheese into small pieces and distribute over the salad, then scatter the toasted buckwheat groats on top.

Pick the small sprigs from the dill stems and sprinkle these over the salad. Trickle over the rapeseed oil and serve at once, before the courgettes become overly soft.

Swaps
Vary the cheese for this dish – a crumbly blue or Wensleydale is particularly good.

Grilled pears and chicory with toasted walnuts

Unlike most other fruit, pears are best harvested before they are fully ripened. If left on the tree, they ripen from the inside and can become overly soft in the middle before the outside is tender. It's one reason why firm pears are all too familiar in our shops. They are, however, ideal for cooking. This is a great autumnal dish that goes exceptionally well with venison; it's equally good served on its own.

Serves 2 as a main, 4 as a side

100g walnuts
3 firm, ripe pears
3 red or white chicory bulbs
50g rocket
50g watercress, tougher stalks
   removed
Juice of 1 orange
Juice of 1 lemon
4 tbsp cold-pressed rapeseed oil
Sea salt and black pepper

If you're cooking outside, heat up the barbecue and allow the fire to die down until the coals are glowing red.

Place a small frying pan over a medium heat on the hob (or on the grill rack), add the walnuts and heat, stirring occasionally, until they start to release their nutty aroma. Tip onto a plate and allow to cool, then break the walnuts up a bit.

If you're cooking indoors, heat a cast-iron griddle pan over a medium-high heat on the hob until smoking hot.

Quarter and core the pears. Cut the chicory bulbs lengthways into quarters.

Place the pears and chicory wedges on the barbecue or in the griddle pan and cook, turning occasionally, until nicely charred on each cut surface. (If you're using a griddle pan you may need to do this in batches.)

Place the charred pears and chicory in a large bowl and add the toasted walnuts, rocket and watercress. Trickle over the citrus juices and rapeseed oil and tumble everything together. Season with salt and pepper to taste. Transfer to a warm platter and serve straight away.

Swaps
Exchange the nuts for a mixture of toasted pumpkin and sunflower seeds.

Kohlrabi, chard, blackcurrants and goat's cheese

Blackcurrants grow in abundance at River Cottage but they are only at their best for a couple of weeks so we freeze them in order to enjoy them for more of the year. They are amazing in savoury food, bringing a deep wine flavour, as well as giving all of the sharpness you need to dress the veg.

Serves 2 as a main, 4 as a side

2 medium or 1 large kohlrabi
100g small chard or spinach leaves
100g blackcurrants (fresh or frozen and thawed)
3 tbsp cold-pressed rapeseed oil
100g soft organic goat's cheese, broken into pieces
A bunch of dill (30g)
Sea salt and black pepper

Peel the kohlrabi and cut in half. Place both halves flat side down on a board and thinly slice into half-moon shapes. Place in a large bowl.

Remove any tougher stalks from the chard or spinach and finely shred the larger leaves. Add to the kohlrabi.

Tip half of the blackcurrants into a small bowl and crush them with the back of a spoon, then add the rapeseed oil and mix well.

Add the crushed blackcurrants to the shredded leaves and kohlrabi and mix well. Leave to stand for 30 minutes, tossing occasionally, then taste and season with salt and pepper. Pick the small sprigs from the dill stems.

Arrange the salad on a serving platter and scatter over the goat's cheese, remaining blackcurrants and the dill sprigs. Serve straight away.

Swaps
Use redcurrants with a little finely diced tender rhubarb in place of the blackcurrants.

Lentils, mustard, watercress and parsley

For a time, lentils were off the menu at River Cottage, simply because they were all imported and we are always on a mission to reduce the impact of our food. That was until our friends at Hodmedods harvested the first British-grown lentils. Thankfully, they've been growing them ever since and lentils are, once again, a firm favourite in some of our most popular dishes.

Serves 2 as a main, 4 as a side

250g English green or Puy lentils
50g Dijon mustard
A bunch of flat-leaf parsley (60g), leaves picked
Juice of 1 lemon
2 tbsp extra virgin olive oil
50ml water
100g watercress, tougher stalks removed
Sea salt and black pepper

Put the lentils into a medium saucepan and cover with cold water. Bring to the boil, lower the heat and cook for 15–18 minutes until they are just cooked but retain a nutty crunch in the middle. Drain the lentils in a sieve, then rinse under cold running water to remove any excess starch. Leave to drain fully.

Tip the lentils into a large bowl and add the mustard, parsley leaves, lemon juice, olive oil and water. Toss to mix and season well with salt and black pepper. (You can refrigerate the lentil salad at this stage for up to 3 days, removing it from the fridge about an hour before you want to eat to bring it to room temperature.)

Just before serving, toss the watercress through the lentil mix. Any leftovers are great fried up and topped with a poached egg for breakfast.

Swaps
Swap the lentils for pearl barley (ideally pre-soaked), increasing the cooking time to 30–35 minutes.

Crispy fried sumac squid, pak choi and bean sprouts

Speed is the key here. As soon as the squid hits the hot pan it will start to toughen so you need to cook it for the shortest time possible over a high heat. It's important to seek out 'jigged' squid, which means it's been caught on lines rather than trawled. You can usually tell if a squid has been trawled – it tends to be sandy.

Serves 2 as a main

500g jigged squid, tubes cleaned,
    tentacles reserved
2 tbsp sunflower oil
1 tbsp sumac
Juice of 1 lemon
20g sesame seeds, toasted
2 tbsp extra virgin olive oil
2 pak choi, divided into leaves
100g bean sprouts
Flaky sea salt and black pepper

Cut the squid tubes into 1cm thick slices and the tentacles into shorter lengths. Put all the squid into a bowl.

Place a cast-iron frying pan or griddle pan over a high heat and wait until it just starts to smoke.

While the pan is heating up, toss the sunflower oil through the squid and season with some flaky sea salt.

Tip the squid into the hot pan, give it 30 seconds and then toss it. Cook for a further minute, no longer, then remove the pan from the heat.

Immediately add the sumac, lemon juice, toasted sesame seeds and olive oil to the squid and mix to combine. Now add the pak choi and bean sprouts and toss together; the leaves should wilt slightly in the heat of the pan.

Taste and add a little salt and pepper if you think it is needed. Transfer to a warm platter and serve straight away, while the salad is still warm.

Swaps
Try replacing the bean sprouts with young spring onions. And if you want to take the salad to the next level, freshly shelled diver-caught scallops are an excellent swap for the squid.

Crab with radishes, orange and watercress

We get the best crabs from the pots of our favourite fisherman, Nigel. He drops them off to us on the way home from his boat and we swiftly dispatch them, then they go straight into the cooking pot. They couldn't be fresher! This salad uses the fine, delicate white meat from the claws and is a regular at our dinners at River Cottage.

Serves 2 as a main, 4 as a starter

200g white crab meat
2 oranges
5 spring radishes, topped and
  tailed
2 tbsp cold-pressed rapeseed oil
50g watercress, tougher stalks
  removed
Sea salt and black pepper

Put the crab meat on a plate and pick through it with your fingertips to check for any fragments of shell, then transfer to a bowl.

Cut a thin slice from the top and bottom of the oranges then stand them on a board and slice off the skin and white pith. Cut the orange segments out from between the membranes and remove any pips. When you're just left with the core of pithy membranes, squeeze this over the crab to release any juice.

Thinly slice the radishes and arrange on a platter with the orange segments. Add the rapeseed oil to the crab meat and mix gently, then taste and season with a little salt and pepper. Distribute the crab over the oranges and radishes, scatter the watercress over the top and serve.

Swaps
This salad is equally delicious prepared with lobster claw and knuckle meat instead of crab.

4
SPICY

This chapter takes you on a fragrant foray that will delight your taste buds. The recipes that follow use heat, smoke and citrus to enhance the aromatics and create stunning flavoured salads that will satisfy and energise you.

Chilli is the most complex of all spices and through this chapter I've employed it in different ways, using smoked as well as fresh chillies. I like to use chilli in a way that's soft and subtle, adding a humming back note of heat without being dominant and overpowering. Capsaicin is what gives chillies their kick; it also helps to stimulate a healthy gut flora, decreasing inflammation in the gut. But chilli is just one of many spices to grace the following pages.

I rarely serve a salad without a finishing crack of freshly ground black pepper – a valuable spice on so many levels. Traders have long referred to it as 'black gold' and it's the world's most traded spice. Compared to chilli, it's fruitier and more rounded in flavour, with a softer back note of heat. Just a modest twist of black pepper over a salad before serving will add visual pop, as well as a flavour lift.

Then you have a parade of spice blends, with merguez definitely being a River Cottage favourite. This North African spice melody comprises cumin, coriander, fennel seed, paprika, cayenne and a generous twist of black pepper. We originally used it exclusively on meat (the blend was initially created for a mutton sausage) but it actually works even better on veg and it gives salads an exotic lift.

I'm also a huge fan of curry powder, which is most certainly not just for curries. It appears in our spiced spelt salad inspired by the flavours of a biryani, featuring spelt with apples and lime (see page 132). But with its earthy notes of cumin and coriander, and sweet hints of cardamon and fennel, you can use medium-heat curry powder to transform a classic potato salad into something more inviting. Try my Curried new potatoes, boiled eggs and watercress (page 147) and you'll see what I mean.

My other favourite salad-lifting spice blends are garam masala, rose harissa and Chinese five-spice. A staple spice paste used in Tunisian dishes, rose harissa is the perfect partner for roast lamb (see the salad on page 155) but equally brilliant mixed with natural yoghurt to make an instant salad dressing. Chinese five-spice is a great partner for rich ingredients like duck (try it in the salad on page 176 in the Lunchbox chapter); it also works well with roasted winter roots or grains like barley.

I love spice so much that I haven't reserved it exclusively for the recipes in this chapter. You'll find aromatic, sweet, hot, invigorating spice peppered throughout the book. I encourage you to be brave, bold and experimental with spice in your salads – adding it to veg, dressings or even offering a final dusting of spice (be it solo or a blend), which is like waving a magic wand over your dishes to make them sparkle.

Spiced spelt salad with apples and lime

This was inspired by a lunch concocted from some leftover takeaway biryani! I added some lettuce, apples and a squeeze of lime to freshen it up and the result was surprisingly light and pleasing. For this refined version I'm using spelt, as it has a great texture and the grains don't stick together in the same way that rice does.

Serves 4 as a main

200g pearled spelt
½ cinnamon stick
25g fresh ginger, cut into slices
1 red chilli, halved lengthways
2 tsp good-quality medium-heat
    curry powder
1 tsp garam masala
2 limes
2 crisp eating apples, such as Gala
    or Cox
2 tbsp cold-pressed rapeseed oil
A small bunch of coriander (30g),
    leaves picked
2 sprigs of mint, leaves picked and
    roughly torn
50g lamb's lettuce or Lollo Rosso
Sea salt and black pepper

Put the spelt into a large saucepan with the cinnamon, ginger, chilli, curry powder and garam masala. Add the juice of ½ lime and toss in the squeezed half-lime shell as well. Pour on enough water to cover the spelt by around 5cm. (You can always top it up halfway through cooking if necessary.) Bring to a simmer and simmer for 15–20 minutes until the spelt is just cooked.

Drain the spelt in a sieve, picking out and discarding the cinnamon, ginger, chilli and lime shell. Set aside to cool to room temperature.

Squeeze the juice from the remaining 1½ limes. Quarter, core and chop the apples into roughly 1cm cubes and place in a large bowl with the spelt. Add the lime juice and rapeseed oil, season with salt and pepper, and toss to combine.

Transfer the spelt mix to a platter and scatter over the coriander, mint and lamb's lettuce. Toss lightly and serve.

Swaps

Try using pearled barley or brown rice in place of the spelt, adjusting the cooking times accordingly. The salad is also delicious if you use olive green or Puy lentils in place of the spelt.

Haricot beans, radicchio, smoked chilli and orange

Having a decent storecupboard is essential. With just a couple of fresh ingredients, it enables you to knock up something quite wonderful, filling and satisfying. And this flavourful salad takes those emergency tins of beans to the next level. It's quite fiery, but if you want to take the heat down you can simply reduce the amount of chilli flakes.

Serves 2 as a main, 4 as a lunch

2 x 400g tins organic white haricot beans, drained and rinsed
2 oranges
2 tsp dried chipotle chilli flakes
1 tsp smoked paprika
2 tsp sweet paprika
2 tbsp extra virgin olive oil
Juice of 1 lime
½ small radicchio, finely shredded
A small bunch of coriander (30g), leaves picked
Sea salt and black pepper

Put the haricot beans into a large bowl. Cut a thin slice from the top and bottom of the oranges then stand them on a board and slice off the skin and white pith. Cut the orange segments out from between the membranes, removing any pips.

Add the orange segments to the beans. When you're just left with the pithy centre of the orange, squeeze it over the bowl to release any remaining juice.

Add the chilli flakes, smoked and sweet paprika, the olive oil and lime juice. Toss to combine and season with salt and pepper to taste.

Finally, toss the radicchio and coriander through the salad and serve immediately, before the leaves start to wilt.

Swaps
You can use any tins of beans or chickpeas you happen to have in the cupboard. A mix of leftover cooked pulses works nicely too.

Roast cauliflower with pumpkin seed satay

As I was growing up, like most children, I had a few foods which I really couldn't get on with – cauliflower was top of that list. Through my career as a chef, I've put a lot of effort into trying to overcome the aversion, and this way of preparing my old nemesis is my favourite. If it could convert me into a cauliflower lover that should be testament enough!

Serves 4 as a main

2 medium cauliflowers (about 750g in total)
3 tbsp cold-pressed rapeseed oil
Flaky sea salt and black pepper

For the satay sauce
Finely grated zest and juice of 1 lime
1 tsp honey
1 tbsp tamari (or soy sauce)
1 tbsp curry powder
3 tbsp pumpkin seed butter or any nut butter (peanut is good)
400ml tin coconut milk

To serve
1 Little Gem lettuce, divided into leaves
5 sprigs of mint, leaves picked and roughly torn
A small bunch of coriander (30g), leaves picked and roughly chopped

Preheat the oven to 210°C/Fan 190°C/Gas 6½. Halve the cauliflowers and remove the tough central cores, then cut into large florets.

Put the cauliflower florets on a baking tray, trickle over the rapeseed oil and season with flaky salt and black pepper. Tumble the cauliflower to coat it in the oil and seasoning, then roast in the oven for 10 minutes, turning the pieces halfway through.

Meanwhile, make the satay sauce. Put the lime zest and juice, honey, tamari, curry powder, pumpkin seed butter and coconut milk into a saucepan and heat gently for 5 minutes, stirring continually to combine.

Take the cauliflower out of the oven, pour on the satay sauce and roll the florets in the sauce until thoroughly coated. Return to the oven for 5 minutes.

Add the lettuce leaves, scatter over the herbs and toss together. Serve immediately.

Swaps
Chunks of root vegetables are a great swap for the cauliflower; parsnips and swede are particularly good. You'll need to roast them for an extra 15 minutes or so before tossing in the satay sauce.

Merguez roast squash, pears and chicory

Merguez is the most used spice blend at River Cottage. It's excellent with squash here, but also incredible with cauliflower (see below) and any roast meat. You'll have more than you need for this recipe, so keep the rest in a jar in your spice cupboard for other uses.

Serves 4 as a main

For the merguez spice mix
1 tsp cumin seeds
1 tsp caraway seeds
1 tsp coriander seeds
1 tsp fennel seeds
1 tsp paprika
A pinch of cayenne pepper

For the roasted veg
1kg squash, such as butternut
   or ½ Crown Prince
2 tbsp extra virgin olive oil
2 red or white chicory bulbs
2 firm, ripe pears
Juice of 1 orange
Juice of 1 lime
Sea salt and black pepper

Preheat the oven to 200°C/Fan 180°C/Gas 6.

First, prepare the merguez spice mix. Scatter all the spice seeds on a baking tray and toast in the oven for 5–8 minutes until they take on a little colour. Leave to cool slightly.

Using a pestle and mortar, roughly grind the toasted spices, retaining a little texture. Add the paprika, cayenne and a couple of twists of the pepper mill. Mix thoroughly.

Peel the squash, cut into large chunks and put into a large roasting tin. Trickle over the olive oil, sprinkle with a generous amount of the merguez spice and season with a little salt. Toss to coat the squash chunks in the oil and spice mix. Roast in the oven at 200°C/Fan 180°C/ Gas 6 for 15 minutes.

Meanwhile, cut the chicory lengthways into quarters. Peel, quarter and core the pears. Add the pear and chicory quarters to the roasting tin, toss with the squash and roast in the oven for a further 8–10 minutes,

Remove from the oven, trickle the orange and lime juice over the roasted veg and pears, and toss gently to mix. Taste to check the seasoning then serve.

Swaps
Peeled chunks of marrow and cauliflower florets are great substitutes for the squash. You'll need to reduce the roasting time a bit for both options.

Spicy, nutty quinoa

Quinoa is a tough grain to get right: undercook it and it's gritty; take it a little too far and it becomes wet and insipid. But, if you catch it at its sweet spot, it retains a little 'pop' and a true nutty flavour. The trick is to use three times as much water as quinoa, and to keep a close eye on the grain as it cooks, stirring occasionally and checking it doesn't boil dry. This should give you delicious, fluffy quinoa every time. Here it pairs beautifully with toasted spices and nuts, fresh chilli, radicchio and parsley in a lemony dressing.

Serves 2 as a main, 4 as a side

1 tsp cumin seeds
1 tsp coriander seeds
1 tsp fennel seeds
50g almonds (skin on), roughly
    chopped
50g hazelnuts (skin on), roughly
    chopped
50g walnuts, roughly chopped
200g quinoa, well rinsed
1 medium-hot red chilli, deseeded
    and finely chopped
½ radicchio, finely sliced
2 tbsp cold-pressed rapeseed oil
Juice of 2 lemons
50g flat-leaf parsley, leaves picked
Sea salt and black pepper

Toast all the seeds in a dry frying pan over a medium heat until they start to release their aroma. Tip into a mortar, cool slightly then bash with the pestle to break them up a bit. Put the pan back on the hob and add all the chopped nuts. Toast until they take on a little colour and smell fragrant. Remove from the heat and allow to cool.

Tip the quinoa into a saucepan, add water to cover and a little salt. Bring to a simmer and cook for around 10–15 minutes, but start testing after 6–7 minutes as it's easy to overcook this grain. It's ready when it's just softened and puffed up (it will start to open up and look a little curly).

Drain off any excess water, then spread the quinoa out on a baking tray and let cool, stirring occasionally to stop it clumping together and overcooking in the residual heat.

Tip the cooled quinoa into a bowl and add the toasted nuts and seeds, fresh chilli and radicchio. Trickle over the rapeseed oil and lemon juice, then toss everything together. Season with salt and pepper to taste.

Transfer the salad to a shallow serving bowl and scatter over the parsley to serve.

Swaps
Switch out the nuts for a mix of pumpkin and sunflower seeds. This salad is also very good made with lentils instead of quinoa.

Broccoli with chilli and pumpkin seeds

You can't get more River Cottage than this one-pan wonder! It's a dish that allows the ingredients to be enjoyed at their best. You can eat it hot, warm or cold – and any leftovers will be good the next day. Sautéeing the broccoli ensures it remains crunchy, and the hint of chilli heat and nutty crunch from the pumpkin seeds round the dish off perfectly. Make sure you have everything prepped and ready before you start cooking.

Serves 2 as a main, 4 as a side

1 head of broccoli
50g pumpkin seeds
2 tbsp light rapeseed oil
1 garlic clove, finely sliced
Finely grated zest and juice of
    1 lemon
1 medium-hot chilli, deseeded
    and thinly sliced
A small bunch of coriander, leaves
    picked and finely chopped
Sea salt and black pepper

Cut the broccoli into florets, leaving a decent amount of stalk on each, then cut each floret into 5mm slices, cutting through the stalk so the broccoli doesn't disintegrate.

Place a large sauté pan over a medium heat, add the pumpkin seeds and toast until they take on a little colour. Tip onto a plate and set aside.

Place the pan back over a high heat. Once it starts to smoke a little, add the rapeseed oil, followed by the broccoli. Cook, stirring constantly, until the broccoli is tinged golden brown.

Now add the garlic, lemon zest and sliced chilli and cook, stirring, for a couple of minutes. Take off the heat and add the pumpkin seeds, coriander and lemon juice. Season with salt and pepper to taste, mix thoroughly and serve.

Swaps
Try a mix of similarly sliced veg, such as cauliflower, carrot and fennel.

Fennel with chilli, lemon and dill

I've been making this salad for as long as I can remember. It's beautifully clean and crunchy with a good chilli kick at the end. Perfect for a hot summer's day or to accompany some fish straight off the barbecue, it's as versatile as it is delicious. Take your time slicing the fennel – getting nice, thin slices is the key here.

Serves 4 as a side

2 fennel bulbs
1 medium-hot red chilli, deseeded
   and finely sliced
Juice of 2 lemons
A small bunch of dill, sprigs picked
   and finely chopped
Sea salt and black pepper

Trim the hard stalks from the top of the fennel and remove any of the root that has discoloured (these trimmings are great for stocks and soups so don't throw them away!).

Cut the fennel bulbs vertically into quarters and finely slice the fennel from the top down, using a mandoline if you have one, making sure the slices are no more than 5mm thick.

Place the fennel slices in a large bowl. Add the chilli, lemon juice and dill and toss all the ingredients together well. Season with salt and pepper to taste then serve.

Swaps
Use ribboned courgettes in place of the fennel. They are delicious tossed in the lemony dressing, but you'll need to serve the salad as soon as you've dressed the courgette ribbons, before they start to soften.

Curried new potatoes, boiled eggs and watercress

When the first of the year's new season potatoes appear in late spring, this is a firm favourite at River Cottage. Their nutty, earthy flavours are a perfect match for the warm spices and bitter watercress, and what isn't made better by a slightly runny egg?

Serves 2 as a main, 4 as a starter

For the pickled onion
1 small red onion
100ml cider vinegar
100ml water
1 tsp coriander seeds
1 tsp fennel seeds
1 tsp cumin seeds

For the salad
1kg new season or baby potatoes (skin on)
4 medium eggs (at room temperature)
1 tsp fennel seeds
1 tsp coriander seeds
3 tbsp olive oil
2 garlic cloves, thinly sliced
1 tbsp medium-hot curry powder
A bunch of watercress, tougher stalks removed
Flaky sea salt and black pepper

For the pickled onion, finely slice the onion into rings and put into a bowl. Put the rest of the ingredients into a pan and add a pinch of salt. Slowly bring to the boil over a low heat to infuse the liquid with the spices, then strain through a sieve into a jug to remove the seeds. Pour the hot liquor over the onion slices to cover and leave to cool.

Place the potatoes in a pan of lightly salted cold water, bring to the boil and cook for 12–15 minutes until just tender. Drain in a colander and allow to dry and cool.

Meanwhile, bring a medium pan of water to the boil. Lower the eggs into the water and cook for 6 minutes, then remove them and immediately immerse in a bowl of iced water to stop the cooking process.

Roughly crush the fennel and coriander seeds, using a pestle and mortar. Place a shallow frying pan over a low heat and add the olive oil, followed by the garlic and crushed spice seeds. Cook, stirring constantly, until golden brown, then add the curry powder and cook for a further minute. Remove from the heat and allow to cool.

Once cooled, halve or quarter the potatoes and toss in the curry mix to coat. Toss the watercress through and transfer to a serving dish. Peel and halve the eggs, season with a little salt and pepper, then place on the salad. Finish with a scattering of drained pickled onion.

Note The pickled onion will keep immersed in the pickling liquor in a jar, in the fridge for up to 3 weeks, and is a great addition to any salad.

Mussels, fennel, chilli and cucumber

We should all eat more mussels. Rope-grown mussels are one of the truly sustainable foods produced in the UK and they are delicious. This is a great way to serve them – you deal with the fiddly shelling as you prepare the salad rather than when you eat them, so you can enjoy them all the more.

Serves 4 as a main

1kg rope-grown mussels,
   de-bearded and rinsed under
   cold running water
350ml dry cider
1 medium fennel bulb
½ cucumber
1 medium-hot red chilli, deseeded
   and finely sliced
Finely grated zest and juice
   of 2 limes
A bunch of basil (50g), leaves
   picked

Check over the mussels, discarding any that are open and don't close when tapped. Heat a large saucepan over a high heat until it starts to smoke. Add the mussels, pour in the cider and immediately put a tight-fitting lid on. Cook for 3 minutes, shaking the pan after 2 minutes. Lift the lid and check that most of the mussels have opened; if not, put the lid back on and cook for a further minute.

Drain the mussels in a sieve over a bowl to catch the juice. Let them cool, then tip into a clean bowl, cover and place in the fridge. Pour the reserved mussel juice through a cloth-lined sieve into a bowl to filter out any bits of shell or grit, then cover and refrigerate.

Quarter the fennel bulb and remove the hard stem base and stalk. Slice from the stalk end as finely as possible and place in a bowl. Quarter the cucumber lengthways and cut into slices the same thickness as the fennel. Add to the bowl with the chilli and lime zest and juice.

Add the mussel juice, then taste and season with pepper and a little salt if needed (the mussel juice will add salt).

Take the mussels from the fridge and discard any that are unopened. Pull the mussels from their shells and stir them through the fennel mix. Roughly tear the basil into the salad and give it a final mix. Have spoons to hand and some sourdough baguette to mop up the delicious liquor.

Swaps
If you can get some cockles or clams, try using in place of the mussels. You will need twice the amount as the shell to flesh ratio is a lot less than with mussels.

Beetroot, sea bass, blackberries and chilli

Curing – rather than cooking – sea bass gives the flesh a beautiful bouncy texture. The acid from the blackberries helps cut through the richness and the almost addictive hit of chilli keeps you coming back for more.

Serves 2 as a main, 4 as a starter

1 fillet of wild sea bass (or bream), rod-and-line caught (about 250g)
200g fine sea salt
6 golf-ball-sized or 2 medium beetroot
20 ripe blackberries
1 medium-hot red chilli, deseeded and finely chopped
3 sprigs of mint, roughly torn
4 sprigs of dill, torn into small sprigs, plus an extra couple to garnish
Sea salt and black pepper

Check the bass fillet for pin bones with your fingertips, pulling out any you find with your fingers or tweezers. Spread half the salt out over a plate, lay the bass fillet skin side down on the salt, then sprinkle the remaining salt on top of the fish. Place in the fridge to cure for 20 minutes.

Remove the sea bass from the fridge and rinse the salt off under cold running water. Pat the fish dry with a clean cloth and return, uncovered, to the fridge.

Put the beetroot into a saucepan, add cold water to cover and bring to the boil. Lower the heat and cook until the beetroot are just tender (insert a small knife to test). Smaller beetroot will take about 20–25 minutes; for larger ones, you'll need to allow up to 45 minutes. Drain and let cool slightly, then rub off the skin. Leave the peeled beetroot to cool completely, then slice into thin wedges.

Next, skin the bass: place the fillet side down on a board and make a small incision 5mm from the tail end, down to the skin but not through it. Grip the skin at that end and use a sharp knife to cut along the skin towards the wider end, separating the flesh from the skin; discard the skin.

Cut the bass flesh into thin slices about the thickness of a £1 coin and place in a bowl. Take half of the blackberries and crush them in your hands over the bass. Add the chilli, mint and dill and mix thoroughly. Place in the fridge to marinate for 20–30 minutes.

Take the bass from the fridge and toss with the beetroot. Season with a little salt and pepper to taste. Finish with the remaining whole blackberries and sprigs of dill.

Leftover lamb, harissa and char-grilled peppers

If, like me, you rarely have any roast lamb left over, it's well worth getting hold of a half shoulder of lamb – or hogget or mutton – to enjoy this North African-inspired delight. I love the harissa heat, but feel free to dial it back to suit your taste.

Serves 4 as a main

300g leftover roast lamb shoulder, torn into pieces, or ½ shoulder of lamb, hogget or mutton, on the bone
1 tbsp organic dried seaweed flakes
1 tbsp rose harissa
1 red pepper
1 green pepper
2 Little Gem lettuce
Juice of 1 lemon
2 tbsp extra virgin olive oil
A small bunch of coriander (30g), leaves picked and roughly chopped
Flaky sea salt and black pepper

If you are cooking fresh lamb, preheat the oven to 170°C/ Fan 150°C/Gas 3. Season the lamb shoulder with salt and pepper, place in a roasting dish, cover with foil and cook for 2–3 hours until the meat is soft and falling apart. Allow the lamb to cool a little then pull the meat from the bones and tear into chunks.

Heat the oven to 200°C/Fan 180°C/Gas 6. Put the leftover or cooked meat into a bowl and add the seaweed and harissa. Toss through the cooked meat and season with a little salt. Spread the meat out on a baking tray and cook in the oven for 10–15 minutes until it takes on some colour.

Heat a cast-iron griddle pan over a high heat until it is smoking hot or heat up your barbecue and let the fire die down a bit.

Halve, core and deseed the peppers then cut each half lengthways into 3 pieces. Cut each lettuce into 6 wedges.

Place the peppers and lettuce wedges on the griddle pan or on the barbecue and cook, turning as necessary, to char on all sides.

Transfer the charred veg to a large bowl. Add the lamb, lemon juice and olive oil and gently mix together. Season with flaky salt, scatter over the coriander and serve.

Swaps
Courgettes and aubergine are great alternatives to the peppers; cook them until charred and tender.

5
LUNCHBOX

With increasingly busy schedules and flexible working patterns, lunch is often overlooked during the week. When we're rushed off our feet, it's all too easy to grab convenience food to keep us going – fillers that are not necessarily healthy. The recipes in this chapter will help you to ditch the 'meal deal', and instead fill your lunchbox with vibrant, fresh food to fuel you through the day.

There are so many incentives to whip up some lunchbox magic and among the most compelling are the brain-boosting benefits. A well-balanced, nutrient-dense salad can help you maintain a sharp focus. Salads are packed with a rainbow of fruits and vegetables, which offer a host of health-boosting vitamins to keep our minds and bodies nourished. I've also embraced the power of protein in this chapter, as it's a key component to a sustaining salad. Protein-rich foods like lentils, seeds, beans and meat (ideally organic) help to maintain energy levels and concentration through the day.

Another thing I love about my lunchbox routine is the fact that it helps me re-energise leftovers. Lentils with green herbs and lemon (page 160) is not only a great way of using up pulses you might have lingering from a previous meal, but also a bed for adding other delicious morsels of roast chicken or beef, or roasted veg. Honey-glazed leftover belly pork with shredded summer veg (page 180) is so good it might just inspire a Sunday pork belly roast tradition, just so you can make this salad to take to work the next day!

Leftover potatoes are perfect in lunchbox salads. Every time I buy a batch of bite-sized spuds, I cook up extra, just so I can make Bacon, new potatoes and lettuce with chunky tartare dressing (page 178). It's also a brilliant way to use leftover bacon (if there is such a thing), which you can crisp further in the oven. I always double the tartare sauce, too, so I can have it with dinner the following night – alongside local fish and a simple leafy salad.

Developing a habit of creating homemade food to tote to work has endless benefits. You'll save money. You'll have more time to eat your lunch as you will skip the queues for substandard take-out food. You're also less likely to be tempted by unhealthy foods. More so, you can pack the food you really like, rather than settle for whatever is available. I love these recipes, because they're so adaptable and satisfying. I think you'll fall for them, too, and I hope they reinvigorate your weekday lunch routine.

Lentils with green herbs and lemon

All too often maligned as boring and bland, lentils can be wonderful. The organic variety we use are grown in Sussex and have a light nutty flavour. The secret is to use plenty of herbs – it really helps the lentils shine. This is a wonderfully versatile recipe, so consider making a bigger batch. Any leftovers are great mixed with a few bashed potatoes or a little mash and fried into hash, which is particularly good alongside a couple of poached eggs or as an accompaniment to fish or chicken.

Serves 4 as a main, 6–8 as a side

3 tbsp extra virgin olive oil
1 medium onion, diced
2 medium carrots, diced
2 bay leaves
250g English green or Puy lentils
Juice of 2 lemons
A bunch of mint (30g), leaves
    picked and finely chopped
A bunch of chives (30g), finely
    chopped
A bunch of dill (30g), sprigs picked
    and finely chopped
A bunch of parsley (30g), leaves
    picked and finely chopped
A bunch of coriander (30g), leaves
    picked and roughly torn
A bunch of basil (30g), leaves
    picked and roughly torn
Sea salt and black pepper

Place a medium saucepan over a medium heat and add 1 tbsp olive oil. When it is hot, add the onion, carrots and bay leaves and sweat until the veg start to soften. Add the lentils and pour on enough water to cover.

Bring to a simmer and cook for 15–18 minutes until the lentils are just cooked but retain a nutty bite in the middle. Drain, tip into a bowl and allow to cool.

Add the lemon juice, remaining olive oil and all of the herbs. Toss to combine and season with salt and pepper to taste before serving.

Swaps
In place of the lentils, try potatoes. Cut into 2cm cubes, toss in 2 tbsp olive oil with the other veg and roast in the oven at 220°C/Fan 200°C/Gas 7 for about 30 minutes.

Roast squash, plums, pumpkin seeds and lime

A great combination of fruity and savoury. Rich, nutty roast squash with slightly caramelised edges is a thing of wonder. In the oven, squash takes on an almost dessert-like sweetness which we counteract here with sharp lime juice to bring it back firmly into the realm of savoury. It's a dish that can be happily made the night before. It's delicious cold – just take it out of the fridge an hour before eating to take the chill off, or reheat in the oven preheated to 210°C/Fan 190°C/Gas 6½ for 10 minutes or so.

Serves 4 as a main, 6 as a side

1kg squash, such as butternut or
    red onion, or ½ Crown Prince
2 tbsp olive oil
300g plums, such as Victoria, or
    damsons, halved and stoned
50g pumpkin seeds
Finely grated zest and juice of
    2 limes
50g tender chard or baby spinach
    leaves
Sea salt and black pepper

Preheat the oven to 200°C/Fan 180°C/Gas 6. Cut the squash into wedges and scoop out the seeds. Place them in a roasting tray, trickle over the olive oil and season with salt and pepper. Toss to coat the squash wedges in the oil and seasoning then roast in the oven for 15 minutes.

Take out the roasting tray, turn the squash wedges, then add the halved plums and scatter over the pumpkin seeds. Return the tray to the oven for 5–10 minutes until the squash is just soft and the plums are still whole but releasing their juices.

Remove the tray from the oven and gently toss through the lime zest and juice, along with the chard or spinach leaves. Taste to check the seasoning before serving – either hot or at room temperature.

Swaps
Try using fresh cherries instead of plums; they lend a decadent, rich flavour to the squash.

Speedy, herby, lemony beans

A super-quick meal. All the herbs are interchangeable here, but the key is to include lots of them. When you think you have enough, add a little more! This salad can be happily made the night before, so it's ideal when you know you have a hectic day ahead. Make sure you have some crusty bread to hand to mop up all the delicious juices.

Serves 2 as a main, 4 as a side

2 x 400g tins mixed beans, drained and rinsed
½ garlic clove, grated or crushed
1 small red onion, halved and sliced
Juice of 1 large or 2 smaller lemons
4 tbsp extra virgin olive oil
A bunch of parsley, leaves picked
A bunch of basil, leaves picked
A bunch of chives
Sea salt and black pepper

Drain the beans thoroughly after rinsing and tip them into a bowl. Add the garlic, red onion, lemon juice, olive oil and some salt and pepper. Tumble everything together to combine.

Finely chop all of the herbs and add them to the beans. Mix through and then taste to check the seasoning.

Serve the salad at room temperature, rather than chilled from the fridge.

Swaps
During the summer months, try a fresher version, using lightly blanched green beans in place of the tinned beans.

Barley, rocket pesto, Cheddar and chives

This is a really enticing combination of flavours. Using rocket for the pesto adds a lovely mustard heat to the barley, and it's balanced with parsley so the pesto doesn't taste bitter. It's a great pesto recipe to have up your sleeve – perfect for dressing salads and finishing, pastas, risottos or pizzas. Make a double batch, pop some in a sterilised jar and cover with a film of olive oil, then it will keep in the fridge for up to a week.

This salad is ideal for making in advance. You can prepare it the night before and have it waiting for you whenever you need it the next day. Just get it out of the fridge an hour or so before serving.

Serves 2 as a main, 4 as a side

200g pearled barley or spelt,
   ideally pre-soaked (for at least
   20 minutes, preferably overnight)
30g chives, cut into 3cm lengths
150g mature Cheddar

For the rocket pesto
100g flat-leaf parsley, leaves picked
50g wild rocket
1 small garlic clove, peeled
100ml extra virgin olive oil
50g pumpkin seeds, lightly toasted
Juice of 1 lemon
Sea salt and black pepper

Put the pearled barley or spelt into a saucepan, cover with water and bring to the boil over a high heat. Lower the heat and simmer until just softened but retaining a little bite: 30–35 minutes for barley; 15–20 minutes for spelt. Remove from the heat and drain in a sieve then rinse under cold running water to remove any excess starch. Transfer to a large bowl.

To make the pesto, put all the ingredients into a food processor and pulse until you have a rough paste. Season with salt and pepper to taste.

Mix the pesto through the barley, then add the chives and tumble through the salad. Break the Cheddar into bite-sized pieces and scatter over the salad. Taste to check the seasoning before serving.

Swaps
Try switching the herbs in the pesto. Basil works well, obviously, or you could also replace some of the parsley with another herb – two-thirds parsley to one-third dill or tarragon is a good mix.

Chickpeas, chicory, lime and chilli

This zingy salad is super quick and packed full of flavour. The chilli and lime add warmth and a citrussy freshness. I use medium-heat chillies, such as jalapeños, rather than a really hot variety, so I can use more of them and get that beautiful pepper flavour as well as some heat. Perfect alongside some simply dressed peppery leaves, this salad is also delicious partnered with roast veg and feta.

Serves 2 as a main, 4 as a side

2 x 400g tins chickpeas, drained and rinsed
2 medium-hot red chillies, deseeded and finely sliced
Finely grated zest and juice of 2 limes
2 tbsp cold-pressed rapeseed oil
1 red chicory bulb
Flaky sea salt and black pepper

Drain the rinsed chickpeas thoroughly and tip them into a large bowl. Add the sliced chillies, along with the lime zest and juice. Trickle over the rapeseed oil, season with a twist of pepper and some flaky sea salt and tumble everything together.

Break the chicory into individual leaves, add to the chickpeas and toss gently. Taste to check the seasoning.

Swaps
Use tinned or freshly cooked dried beans in place of the chickpeas – you can use any variety or a mixture. For a less fiery flavour, swap out one of the chillies for a finely diced red pepper.

Dhal salad

This salad is flavoured with all the familiar dhal spices but uses a type of lentil that doesn't break down, so it retains a delicious bite. Vibrant, fresh tomatoes, watercress and spring onion finish it off beautifully. It's a real winner every time and is amazing topped with a fried egg or a generous dollop of natural yoghurt – or a saucy curry if you like.

Serves 2 as a main, 4 as a side

To cook the lentils
250g English green or Puy lentils
1 tsp ground turmeric
½ cinnamon stick
1 red chilli, halved and deseeded
20g fresh ginger, sliced

For the dhal
3 tbsp sunflower oil
1 garlic clove, finely chopped
20g fresh ginger, finely grated
1 red chilli, deseeded and
    finely chopped
1 tsp ground coriander
1 tsp ground cumin
1 tsp garam masala

To assemble
Juice of 1 lemon
50g watercress, tougher stalks
    removed
5 spring onions, finely sliced
2 tomatoes, chopped
Sea salt and black pepper

Put the lentils into a medium saucepan with the turmeric, cinnamon, red chilli and ginger. Pour on enough cold water to cover and bring to the boil. Lower the heat and cook for 15–18 minutes until they are just cooked but retain a nutty crunch in the middle. Drain the lentils in a sieve and remove the chilli, ginger and cinnamon. Leave to drain fully.

To prepare the dhal, place a sauté pan over a low heat and add the sunflower oil. Toss in the garlic, ginger, red chilli, ground coriander, cumin and garam masala and cook, stirring, until the garlic is softened and the spices are releasing their aromas.

Toss the drained lentils through the frying spices and then remove from the heat and leave to cool.

Add the lemon juice, watercress, spring onions and tomatoes to the spiced lentils. Tumble everything together and season with salt and pepper to taste.

Swaps
Tinned chickpeas are a great, speedy alternative to the lentils. You'll need to use 2 x 400g tins.

Roast squash, blackberries, feta and walnuts

Almost everywhere you walk in late summer and autumn you'll come across blackberry bushes bearing fruits, as long as they haven't already been stripped of their harvest by others. The season lasts from late August into October, giving you ample opportunity to collect and freeze lots to last through the winter. Don't just save them for crumbles and pies – they are good in savoury dishes too. Here they pair well with roast squash. If you can get an interesting variety such as Crown Prince or Uchiki Kuri, give it a go as a change from the ubiquitous butternut.

Serves 4 as a main, 6–8 as a side

1kg squash, such as butternut, or ½ Crown Prince or a small Uchiki Kuri
2 tbsp extra virgin olive oil
30 ripe blackberries
60g walnuts, roughly chopped and lightly toasted
½ radicchio, torn into pieces
3–4 sprigs of tarragon, leaves picked
150g feta
Sea salt and black pepper

Preheat the oven to 200°C/Fan 180°C/Gas 6. Peel and deseed the squash and cut into fairly slim wedges or large chunks. If your squash is still quite young you can leave the skin on, as it will be edible. (Young squash that haven't been stored are only available from late August to the end of October.)

Place the squash in a roasting tray, trickle over the olive oil and season with salt and pepper. Toss to coat the squash in the oil and seasoning. Roast in the oven for 15–20 minutes, turning the squash pieces halfway through cooking.

Add half of the blackberries to the roasting tray and mix through the squash, breaking up the berries as you do so. Add the toasted walnuts, radicchio and tarragon and toss to combine.

Roughly crumble the feta on top of the salad, scatter over the remaining blackberries and serve – either hot or at room temperature.

Swaps
A good salty blue cheese, such as a Ticklemore from Devon, is an excellent alternative to the feta. Or for a milder, creamier option, torn mozzarella works a treat.

Green beans, five-spice crispy duck and bean sprouts

Once you've tasted this salad, you'll find an excuse to make it again and again. Lovely and light, with a subtly spiced finish, it's totally delicious. If you are making it in advance to take to work, put the dressing into a separate pot and stir it through the salad when you're ready to eat.

Serves 2 as a main

1 free-range duck leg
1 tsp Chinese five-spice powder
100g green beans, halved
1 tbsp sesame oil
50g bean sprouts
4 spring onions, thinly sliced
1 tbsp sesame seeds

For the dressing
1 tbsp soy sauce
1 tsp honey
Juice of 1 lime

Preheat the oven to 170°C/Fan 150°C/Gas 3. Rub the duck leg all over with the five-spice powder. Place in a small roasting tray and roast for an hour or until you can easily pull the leg bone from the meat. Remove from the oven and turn the setting up to 210°C/Fan 190°C/Gas 6½.

Leave the duck until it is cool enough to handle, then carefully remove all of the bones and roughly shred the meat and skin. Place in a large bowl.

Put the green beans on a baking tray, trickle with the sesame oil and toss to coat. Spread out on the tray and roast in the hot oven for 4–5 minutes until just starting to become tender. Remove from the oven; allow to cool.

Add the cooled beans to the duck, along with the bean sprouts, spring onions and sesame seeds.

For the dressing, in a separate bowl, mix the soy, honey and lime juice together. If you're not eating straight away, put the dressing into a screw-topped jar and seal.

Just before you eat, add the dressing to the duck salad and mix it through thoroughly.

Swaps
For a brilliant vegetarian version, replace the duck with organic tofu. Cut a 400g block of extra-firm tofu into 2–3cm cubes. Sprinkle the tofu with the five-spice and some salt and pepper, toss in a little sesame oil and spread out on a shallow roasting tray. Roast at 200°C/Fan 180°C/Gas 6 for 25–30 minutes.

Bacon, new potatoes and lettuce with chunky tartare dressing

This is one of my absolute favourites. The saltiness of the bacon seasoning the crispy potatoes with a good helping of the indulgent dressing makes it irresistible. The tartare dressing is great with lots of other things – especially barbecued or grilled mackerel and sardines.

Serves 2 as a main, 4 as a side

500g new potatoes (skin on)
150g good-quality dry-cure streaky bacon, derinded and roughly diced
A splash of light rapeseed oil (if needed)
1 Little Gem lettuce, divided into leaves

For the tartare dressing
2 medium eggs
150g cucumber
A few sprigs of flat-leaf parsley, leaves picked
A few sprigs of dill, leaves picked, plus extra sprigs to finish
2 tsp capers, drained and rinsed
100g good-quality mayonnaise (for homemade see page 215)

Put the potatoes into a saucepan, cover with cold water and bring to the boil. Lower the heat and cook for 15–20 minutes or until the potatoes are just cooked. Drain and leave to steam-dry in the colander until cool enough to handle. Halve the potatoes; cut larger ones into quarters.

Meanwhile, for the dressing, bring a medium pan of water to the boil. Lower the eggs into the water and cook for 6 minutes, then remove them and immediately immerse in a bowl of iced water to stop the cooking process.

Roughly dice the cucumber into 1cm cubes and place in a bowl. Roughly chop the parsley, dill and capers together then add to the cucumber. Peel and roughly chop the boiled eggs and add to the bowl with the mayonnaise. Mix well and taste the dressing to check the seasoning.

Add the bacon to a cold heavy-based frying pan and place over a low heat to draw out the fat. Cook the bacon until it crisps nicely, then remove it from the pan with a slotted spoon and place in a large serving bowl.

Add the potatoes to the fat remaining in the pan and fry, turning occasionally, until crisp at the edges (if necessary, add a little oil). Drain the potatoes on kitchen paper.

Add the potatoes and lettuce to the bacon, toss to mix and spoon on the dressing. Finish with a scattering of dill.

Swaps
Use peppery mizuna or watercress instead of lettuce. For a veggie version, replace the bacon with pitted Kalamata olives (fry the potatoes in a little oil to crisp them).

Honey-glazed leftover belly pork with shredded summer veg

Sticky and delicious, this is a comfort blanket of a meal! The pork pairs so well with the crunchy shredded raw veg and the intense flavours of the tamari, lime and honey bring the two together brilliantly. This will quickly become a lunchtime favourite.

Serves 2, as a generous lunch

300g leftover roast pork or
   a 500g piece of pork belly
2 tbsp honey
2 tbsp tamari (or soy sauce)
2 tsp sesame seeds
Juice of 2 limes
1 small red onion
1 carrot
1 small courgette
50g mangetout
½ red chilli, deseeded and
   finely diced
100g bean sprouts

If you're cooking a piece of pork belly, preheat the oven to 180°C/Fan 160°C/Gas 4. Place the pork in a roasting tray, add a little water or stock to the tray, cover with foil and cook for 1½–2 hours or until the pork is falling apart. Remove from the oven and let cool slightly.

Tear the leftover or freshly cooked pork into rough pieces and place in a bowl. Mix the honey, tamari, sesame seeds and lime juice together in a small bowl and then add to the pork and toss to combine.

Heat the oven to 220°C/Fan 200°C/Gas 7. Spread the pork out in a single layer on a baking tray and place in the oven for 6 minutes. Take it out and turn the pork then return to the oven for another 6 minutes. The pork should be nice and sticky now, but if not return it to the oven for a further 6 minutes, keeping a close eye to make sure that it doesn't burn. Leave to cool.

While the pork is in the oven, slice the onion, carrot, courgette and mangetout into very fine shreds and toss together in a bowl with the chilli and bean sprouts.

About 5 minutes before eating, mix the veg and pork together with any juices left on the baking tray. (If preparing for a lunchbox, pack the pork and veg separately and combine shortly before you eat.) It's a salad best eaten at room temperature, so if you make it ahead, take it from the fridge an hour or so before eating.

Swaps
You can use any leftover meat for this salad; leftover chicken leg meat is a particularly good alternative.

6
RIVER COTTAGE CLASSICS

This chapter is all about River Cottage takes on classic salads, such as tabbouleh, coleslaw, Waldorf salad, panzanella and salade niçoise. These recipes have stood the test of time, but still lend themselves perfectly to creative variations.

The Waldorf, which takes its name from the Waldorf-Astoria hotel in New York City, is one of my favourites. The original recipe comprised just four ingredients: apple, celery, mayonnaise and lettuce; walnuts were a later addition. I have included shredded Brussels sprouts, for a winter twist, and nuggets of tangy West Country Cheddar (see page 190). You'll be surprised how good this combination tastes!

Panzanella is a legendary Italian salad, featuring stale chunks of ciabatta, flavourful tomatoes and cucumber. The bread absorbs the juices from the tomatoes and extra virgin olive oil dressing – to delicious effect. Sourdough is a great swap for ciabatta here. I've also included summer berries in the mix – their juices further help to soften the bread and they lend a delicious sweetness (see page 193).

Salade niçoise is another classic that I adore. In fact, this famous French salad began its life as a sandwich (it was more like a pan bagnat). The great French chef Auguste Escoffier got his hands on the recipe and radically shifted it into salad territory. He raised some serious eyebrows when he decided to include potatoes and green beans. This salad, on many levels, is delightfully contradictory. In equal measure, it consists of ingredients that have been preserved (in a tin or a jar) and items that have only just been harvested. In the recipe on page 203, I've replaced the traditional tuna with more sustainable smoked mackerel.

Having a storecupboard and a fridge stocked with salad ingredients makes it so easy to throw a sumptuous salad together. My go-to staples include hazelnuts, walnuts and almonds; sunflower, sesame and pumpkin seeds; olives, capers, anchovies and kimchi (or Kimkraut, see page 232); feta, goat's cheese and a good Cheddar; plus a selection of dried fruit. Partnered with a handful of leaves and herbs, these dependable standbys will help you to create tasty, nourishing salads in next to no time.

Be it a new dish or our spin on a time-honoured recipe, every River Cottage dish follows the ethos SLOW: seasonal, local, organic and wild. These are principles that we use when we create dishes at River Cottage, opting for produce at its peak, grown without chemical inputs on farms near you – or even better, grown by you. These are the things that really transform a dish and offer a springboard to reproduce some brilliant classics – be it by the book or with a seasonal twist or a quirky play on words that leads to a delightful new taste discovery, like when we put a new 'kohl' in coleslaw (see page 189) or turned a classic sandwich (the BLT) into a mouth-watering salad (see page 208).

Barley tabbouleh

Our version of this Middle Eastern classic uses pearl barley rather than the classic bulgur wheat, to excellent effect. Often used as an afterthought to bulk out soups and stews, barley deserves to take centre-stage more often. It works well here and, with the addition of a crunchy eating apple, gives the salad a distinctly British twist.

Serves 4 as a main, 6–8 as a side

250g pearl barley, ideally
    pre-soaked (for at least
    20 minutes, preferably overnight)
½ cucumber
1 crisp eating apple, such as
    Cox or Gala
15 ripe cherry tomatoes, halved
4 spring onions, finely sliced
1 garlic clove, finely chopped
    or grated
Juice of 1 lemon
Juice of 1 lime
3 tbsp cold-pressed rapeseed oil
A small bunch of flat-leaf parsley
    (30g)
A small bunch of mint (30g)
A small bunch of coriander (30g)
Sea salt and black pepper

Put the pearl barley into a saucepan, cover with cold water and bring to the boil over a high heat. Lower the heat and simmer for about 30–35 minutes until just softened but retaining a bite. Remove from the heat and drain in a sieve then rinse under cold running water to remove any excess starch. Leave to cool.

In the meantime, cut the cucumber into 5mm cubes. Quarter, core and chop the apple.

Tip the cooled pearl barley into a large bowl and add the cucumber, apple, cherry tomatoes, spring onions and garlic. Trickle in the lemon and lime juices and the rapeseed oil and tumble the ingredients together. Season with salt and pepper to taste.

Pick the herb leaves from their stems, roughly chop or tear them and toss through the salad. Enjoy!

Swaps
For a different take on this vibrant fresh-tasting salad, replace the barley with quinoa or lentils, adjusting the cooking time accordingly.

Kohl slaw

This take on one of the best-known salads in the world stemmed from our love of a play on words at River Cottage and it turned out to be fabulous! Kohlrabi is a vegetable that's become much more widely available. Literally translating as 'turnip cabbage' it has a fresh cabbage-y flavour with a hint of apple. Shredded and tossed with carrot, spring onions and apple, and lightly dressed with lemon and olive oil, it is transformed into a much lighter version of the enduring classic salad.

Serves 4 as a side

1 large kohlrabi (about 400g)
1 large carrot (about 100g)
3 spring onions
1 crisp eating apple, such as
   Cox or Gala
Juice of 1 lemon
2 tbsp extra virgin olive oil
A small bunch of flat-leaf parsley
   (30g)
Sea salt and black pepper

Peel the kohlrabi and slice into 3mm thick slices, then cut across the slices to achieve long thin julienne. Peel the carrot and cut into similar-sized julienne or grate coarsely. Finely slice the spring onions on an angle. Combine the veg in a large bowl.

Quarter, core and dice the apple into 1cm cubes. Add to the veg with the lemon juice and olive oil and tumble everything together. Season with salt and pepper to taste.

Pick the leaves from the parsley stems and finely chop them, then toss through the salad. Taste to check the seasoning before serving.

Swaps
Finely sliced fennel is a gorgeous substitute for the kohlrabi. You'll need to use a medium fennel bulb.

Brussels sprout Waldorf

Eating sprouts raw opens up a whole new way of thinking about them! The key to nailing this salad is to cut the sprouts nice and finely. The first time I made it for a group of people, everyone was sceptical... until they tasted it. Thankfully, the entire bowl was polished off in no time! The repeated question was, 'Why can't sprouts taste like this all the time?' Simple answer is... they can.

Serves 4 as a main, 8 as a side

500g Brussels sprouts
1 head of celery (about 500g)
2 crisp eating apples, such as Cox or Gala
200g red grapes, halved (any pips removed)
200g walnuts, chopped and lightly toasted
150g mature Cheddar, broken into pieces
3 tbsp good-quality mayonnaise (for homemade see page 215)
3 tbsp natural yoghurt
A bunch of flat-leaf parsley (30g)
Sea salt and black pepper

To prepare the sprouts, trim off a little of the root end where it is discoloured and peel away any discoloured or damaged outer leaves, but don't be overzealous – the dark green leaves are delicious. Cut the sprouts in half lengthways through the root, lay flat cut side down on a board and slice from the top down, as thinly as you can. Put the shredded sprouts into a large bowl.

Separate the celery sticks and slice them across into 1cm thick slices. Add to the shredded sprouts.

Quarter, core and chop the apples into 1cm cubes and add to the bowl with the grapes, walnuts, cheese, mayonnaise and yoghurt. Mix the ingredients together well and season with salt and pepper to taste.

Pick the leaves from the parsley stalks, finely chop them and stir through the salad. Serve straight away.

Swaps

Celeriac is a great alternative to the sprouts – you'll need to cut it into very fine julienne. For a lighter dressing, omit the mayo and double the quantity of yoghurt.

Panzanella

I couldn't write a book about salads without including a recipe for panzanella; it's such a wondrous thing. At River Cottage, we like to include a little fruit, as it enhances the flavour of the tomatoes. Strawberries are my favourite addition, but gooseberries and raspberries are good too.

Serves 2 as a main, 4 as a side

2 slices of slightly stale sourdough
   or ciabatta
1kg mixed, slightly over-ripe,
   tomatoes
½ cucumber
1 small red onion, finely diced
1 tbsp capers, drained, rinsed
   and roughly chopped
100g Kalamata olives, pitted
150g halved gooseberries,
   quartered strawberries or
   whole raspberries
3 tbsp extra virgin olive oil
A small bunch of basil (25g),
   leaves picked

Preheat the oven to 200°C/Fan 180°C/Gas 6. Tear the bread into large chunks and scatter on a baking tray. Toast in the oven for 3–5 minutes until crisp and lightly golden, turning once. Remove and allow to cool.

Pick the ripest 2 tomatoes (fairly soft is fine) and squish them in your hands into a sieve set over a large bowl. Using the back of a wooden spoon, press the tomato flesh through the sieve; discard the seeds and skins.

Cut the rest of the tomatoes into wedges or chop them roughly and add to the bowl containing the tomato juice. Dice the cucumber and add to the tomatoes with the red onion, capers, olives, and your choice of fruit.

Toss in the toasted bread chunks and trickle in the olive oil. Roughly tear half of the basil leaves into the salad. Tumble everything together and allow the salad to sit for 15–20 minutes.

Season the panzanella with salt and pepper to taste and give it a final toss. Tear over the remaining basil and serve.

Swaps
If you can get it, try using lovage instead of the basil – it works beautifully. Celery leaves are a good swap too.

Potato salad with apples and Cheddar

As a kid, when I got home from school I used to snack on apples, Cheddar and mayonnaise. It wasn't conventional and my mother was forever wondering where all the mayonnaise was going. As I grew older, I folded this delicious combination in with another favourite – new potatoes – to get the best of both worlds. This remains my go-to dish for any occasion, from picnic to barbecue.

Serves 4 as a main, 8 as a side

200g new potatoes
200g mature Cheddar
2 crisp eating apples
2–3 tbsp good-quality mayonnaise
    (for homemade see page 215)
A bunch of flat-leaf parsley (30g),
    leaves picked
A bunch of chives (30g)
Sea salt and black pepper

Put the new potatoes into a saucepan, cover with cold water and bring to the boil over a high heat. Lower the heat and cook for 15–20 minutes or until the potatoes are just tender through to the centre. Drain and allow to cool.

Cut the potatoes into 2–3cm chunks and place in a large bowl. Cut the cheese into 1–2cm cubes and add to the potatoes. Quarter, core and chop the apples into roughly 2cm chunks and add these to the bowl too.

Add the mayonnaise and tumble everything together. Taste before seasoning with salt and pepper. Finely chop the parsley and chives, scatter these over the salad and toss through before serving.

Swaps
For a potato/Waldorf hybrid salad, leave out the apples and replace with about 80g grapes, halved and deseeded, and a couple of celery sticks, cut into 1cm cubes.

Carrot, cabbage, ginger and chilli slaw

This was first made for one of our staff summer parties almost a decade ago. It was such a big hit that it went on our menus shortly after and has remained there ever since. It's perfect for a summer lunch, or to roll out once the barbecue is fired up, but its accessible ingredients, chilli warmth and aromatic dressing make it a great year-round salad.

Serves 4–6 as a side

¼ red cabbage
¼ white cabbage
1 large carrot
1 medium-hot or mild chilli, to taste, deseeded and finely sliced
A small bunch of chives
10g sesame seeds, toasted

For the tamari and ginger dressing
1 garlic clove, finely grated
25g fresh ginger, finely grated
2 tbsp tamari (or soy sauce)
Finely grated zest and juice of 1 lime

Remove the hard stem base from both cabbage quarters, along with the outer leaf if it is limp or discoloured. Finely slice the cabbages from the pointed end down to the stem base. Put the shredded cabbage into a large bowl.

Peel and coarsely grate the carrot and add to the bowl with the chilli. Chop the chives and add these too, along with the sesame seeds. Tumble everything together.

To make the dressing, put all the ingredients into a small bowl and stir to combine.

Add the dressing to the veg, mix together, then allow the salad to sit for 5 minutes. Toss the salad once more before serving.

Swaps
Try dressing this salad with the Orange, kimchi and seaweed dressing on page 226; it's a revelation.

Fava bean hummus and Little Gem salad

It wouldn't be a River Cottage book without the inclusion of some form of hummus. Made by beating rather than blending the ingredients together, this version has plenty of texture – you may even get the odd whole fava bean as you're eating. The raw lemon may sound a little out there, but if you're careful to remove all the bitter pith, you're in for a real citrussy treat. It's a great hummus to snack on.

Serves 2 as a main, 4 as a starter

500g split dried fava beans
4 garlic cloves, finely grated
4 tbsp extra virgin olive oil,
    plus a little extra to finish
2 tbsp tahini
10g ground cumin
Juice of 1 lemon
Sea salt and black pepper

To assemble and serve
1 lemon
3 Little Gem lettuce, divided into
    leaves
4 sprigs of mint, leaves picked

Put the fava beans into a saucepan and cover with water. Bring to the boil, lower the heat and cook for about 40 minutes until just softened. Drain thoroughly and tip into a large bowl.

Add the garlic, olive oil, tahini, cumin and lemon juice to the warm fava beans and beat with a spoon until you have a rough 'hummus'. Season well with salt and pepper and allow to cool.

Cut a thin slice from the top and bottom of the lemon, then stand it on a board and slice off the skin and pith. Cut out the segments between the membranes then cut these into small pieces, discarding the pips.

Spread the lettuce leaves out over a large serving plate and dollop the hummus all over them. Scatter over the lemon pieces and roughly tear the mint over everything. Trickle a little extra olive oil over the salad and serve.

Swaps
Try using butter beans instead of fava beans, adjusting the cooking time accordingly. For a speedy version you can use tinned butter beans; you'll need 2 x 400g tins.

Smoked mackerel niçoise

Mackerel has long been our favourite fish at River Cottage – through the summer months a day rarely passes when we don't cook it. Tuna is firmly off the menu because of serious overfishing issues, so we use smoked mackerel for our niçoise salad instead. Mackerel is caught around most of the UK coastline from mid-May through until early autumn, and frankly it's better than tuna in this salad. We like to hot-smoke it over oak chips, which suits the oily flesh perfectly.

Serves 2 as a main

200g new potatoes
200g green beans, halved
4 medium eggs (at room temperature)
4 smoked mackerel fillets, skinned
1 banana shallot, finely sliced
4 ripe tomatoes
1 Little Gem lettuce, divided into leaves
100g Kalamata olives, pitted
2 tbsp extra virgin olive oil
Sea salt and black pepper

Place the potatoes in a pan of lightly salted cold water, bring to the boil and cook for 15–18 minutes until almost tender. Add the beans and cook for a further 3 minutes. Drain in a colander and allow to dry and cool.

Meanwhile, bring a medium pan of water to the boil. Lower the eggs into the water and cook for 6 minutes, then remove them and immediately immerse in a bowl of iced water to stop the cooking process. Once cooled, drain and peel the eggs, then cut into quarters.

Halve the potatoes lengthways (or cut into quarters if large) and place in a large bowl, with the beans.

Check the smoked mackerel for pin bones, removing any you find with fingers or tweezers, then flake into chunks and add to the potatoes and beans with the shallot.

Chop the tomatoes into small pieces and add these to the salad. Tear in the lettuce leaves, add the olives and season with salt and pepper to taste. Trickle over the olive oil and tumble everything together.

Divide the salad between serving bowls, add the boiled egg wedges and finish with a few twists of the peppermill.

Swaps
For a vegetarian option, replace the fish with char-grilled, well-seasoned strips of aubergine and/or courgette.

Cheaty chicken Caesar salad

This is up there with the best-known salads in the world and it's a great one for using up the leftovers from a roast chicken. Once the bird has cooled, I find hunting out those juicy morsels extremely satisfying and it always surprises me how much is left nestling against the bones!

Serves 4 as a main

2 slices of sourdough or
   good-quality wholemeal bread,
   crusts removed
2 tbsp olive oil
300g cold leftover chicken, torn
   into pieces
1 Cos lettuce, divided into leaves
8 tinned or jarred anchovy fillets
   (MSC certified)
100g extra mature Cheddar
Flaky sea salt and black pepper

For the Caesar dressing
4 tbsp good-quality mayonnaise
   (for homemade see page 215)
2 tinned or jarred anchovy fillets
   (MSC certified), finely chopped
½ garlic clove, finely grated
30g extra mature Cheddar,
   finely grated

Preheat the oven to 200°C/Fan 180°C/Gas 6. Tear the bread into pieces, toss in the olive oil and season with salt and pepper.

Scatter the bread pieces on a baking tray and bake for 8–10 minutes until golden brown and crisp. Remove from the oven, drain on kitchen paper and allow to cool.

For the dressing, mix all the ingredients together in a bowl, then taste to check the seasoning (the anchovies will probably have contributed enough salt).

Put the chicken and baked bread into a large bowl. Tear each of the lettuce leaves into 2 or 3 pieces and add them to the bowl, then stir through the dressing.

Arrange the salad on a large platter, top with the anchovy fillets and shave the cheese (using a peeler) over the top.

Swaps
For a lighter version, replace the mayonnaise with natural yoghurt and add an extra squeeze of lemon juice to the Caesar dressing.

Russian salad with sardines

Russian salad was first created in Moscow around 150 years ago and has become a classic around the globe. Our River Cottage take sticks pretty close to the original recipe, though we swap turnip for celeriac and green beans for peas. Serving the salad with grilled sardines is our favourite way, but it is good alongside any oily fish.

Serves 2 as a main, 4 as a starter

2 carrots
½ medium celeriac (about 150g)
2 waxy potatoes
10 green beans
3 tbsp good-quality mayonnaise
    (for homemade see page 215)
2 gherkins, finely diced
6 sprigs of flat-leaf parsley,
    leaves picked
8 fresh sardines
2 tbsp olive oil
Sea salt and black pepper
Lemon wedges, to serve

Bring a pan of water with a pinch of salt added to the boil over a high heat. Peel the carrots and celeriac and cut these and the potatoes into 1cm cubes, keeping the celeriac separate. Cut the green beans into 1cm lengths.

Add the potatoes and carrots to the pan and cook for 5 minutes, then add the celeriac and cook until the potatoes just start to soften. Add the beans and cook for another minute. Drain in a colander; leave to cool and dry.

Tip the cooked veg into a large bowl and add the mayo and gherkins. Finely chop the parsley and add to the salad. Tumble everything together and season the salad with a little salt and pepper if you think it is needed.

Preheat the grill to its highest setting. Place the sardines on a sturdy baking tray, trickle over the olive oil and season both sides of the fish with salt and pepper.

Place the baking tray under the grill for 2 minutes and then turn the sardines and cook for a further 2 minutes. Tease open the thickest part of a sardine down to the bone to check it is cooked all the way through. Don't be afraid to get a good colour on the skin.

Serve the grilled sardines with the Russian salad and lemon wedges on the side for squeezing over.

Swaps
For a lighter summer veg version, serve the Russian salad with wedges of grilled Little Gem lettuce and roasted peppers rather than sardines.

BLT salad

All the ingredients of the best-selling sandwich are here but in different proportions and the bread is fried into croûtons to add crunch and character. It makes a lovely light dish to serve as a sharing platter.

Serves 4 as a lunch, 2 as a main

350g heritage tomatoes
1 tbsp extra virgin olive oil
2 tbsp sunflower oil
180g bacon lardons
75g sourdough, torn into
   small pieces
1 medium Cos lettuce, leaves
   separated
3–4 tbsp good-quality mayonnaise
   (for homemade see page 215)
5–6 sprigs of thyme, divided into
   little sprigs
Sea salt and black pepper

Cut the tomatoes into small pieces and place in a bowl with the olive oil and some salt and pepper. Tumble them together and set aside.

Set a heavy-based frying pan over a medium-high heat. Add the sunflower oil, followed by the bacon lardons. Fry gently, turning the lardons until they are golden and starting to crisp. Remove with a slotted spoon and place on some kitchen paper to drain.

Add the pieces of sourdough to the oil remaining in the pan and fry, turning regularly, until golden and crisp. Drain the croûtons on kitchen paper too.

Arrange the lettuce leaves, cup side up, on individual plates. Spoon the chopped tomatoes into the lettuce leaves and scatter over the croûtons and bacon. Add a dollop of mayonnaise to each plate – for dipping the leaves into – and finish with a scattering of thyme.

Swaps
For an all-veg version, switch out the bacon and add around 50g sliced pitted olives and 1–2 tbsp capers, to keep that salty hit.

7
DRESSINGS, PICKLES & KRAUTS

Most salad dressings are a simple yet carefully composed dance between two key culinary components: acid and fat. A classic French vinaigrette will feature red wine vinegar as the acid but there are many alternatives.

Beyond dressing leaves and other salad-destined veg, fruit, grains and pulses, you can also use your homemade dressings to sauce up fish, meat and other dishes. The Soy, lime, chilli and ginger dressing (page 225) is particularly good for enhancing grilled fish and shellfish. Some dressings, like the Lemon and garlic dressing (page 222), also work well as a marinade – the acid helps to tenderise meat. And thicker dressings, like mayonnaise and its derivatives (on pages 215–6), make great dips.

The acid component of your dressing can be a classic wine vinegar (red or white), balsamic or cider vinegar, or herb- or fruit-infused vinegar. Or you can use citrus juice (lemon, lime or any kind of orange); add the zest, too – it has natural oils which make the dressing creamier. A purée of acidic fruits, such as gooseberries, is another option. You can also use sauerkraut brine, kimchi brine or pickle juice, or even kombucha.

As for the oil (or fat) component of your dressing, the options are pretty much endless. Apart from the obvious olive oil, rapeseed, walnut, hazelnut, sesame, pumpkin seed, linseed, hemp and avocado oils all work well. Or, instead of oil, you can use a nut or seed butter, such as cashew, almond, peanut, pumpkin seed or tahini. The oil can even be swapped for a dairy product, such as yoghurt or kefir. And avocado can be blended with any of the acid components for a rich, creamy dressing.

Once you've decided on your acid and fat components, the next step in the salad dressing tango is the ratio. Salad dressings typically contain 3–4 parts fat to 1 part acid. So, for a classic vinaigrette, you whisk 30–40ml olive oil with 10ml vinegar, but these rules are slightly flexible.

Additional elements to a great salad dressing are a hint of sweetness, a touch of salt and the pungency of mustard. Mixing mustard with the vinegar before whisking in the oil can help to stabilise the dressing and it gives a peppery heat. You can add sweetness with a little honey, a drop of maple syrup, or a little date syrup or date purée. And always remember to season your dressing – try using a flavoured sea salt here for a change.

You can take your creativity a step further by blending fresh herbs, such as basil, chives, oregano, lemon balm, tarragon or lemon verbena, into your dressing. Or add a touch of warmth with spices like ground cardamom, cumin or coriander, curry powder, harissa, sumac, chilli and ginger.

The benefits of homemade over shop-bought dressings extend beyond flavour. Most commercial dressings contain emulsifiers and stabilisers, many are high in sugar and salt, and the majority are pasteurised, so you lose out on healthy elements which are destroyed by that process.

Hopefully the ideas that follow will inspire you to get creative. And once you're happy with the dressings you're creating, have fun making the krauts and pickles at the end of this chapter. These will also elevate your salads to the next level.

Mayonnaise

Making your own mayo takes just a few minutes and it is far superior to anything you can buy, so give it a go. This classic dressing is also the base for so many other wonderful things (see below and overleaf).

You can use either extra virgin olive or cold-pressed rapeseed oil, but it's important that this is only half of the oil. The other half needs to be a pretty flavourless oil, so a refined rapeseed or sunflower is ideal.

Fresh mayo does not last as long as the shop-bought stuff so keep it refrigerated and use within a couple of days (it never lasts more than a few hours in my house!).

Makes a 250g jar

2 egg yolks
2 tsp Dijon mustard
2 tsp cider vinegar
Juice of ½ lemon
125ml extra virgin olive oil or
    cold-pressed rapeseed oil
    (at room temperature)
125ml light rapeseed or sunflower
    oil (at room temperature)
Fine sea salt and black pepper

Put the egg yolks, mustard, vinegar and lemon juice into a small food processor and blitz briefly to combine. Then, with the motor running, slowly add the oils, a few drips at a time to start with, then in a thin trickle. The mayo will thicken as more oil is added. (Alternatively, you can make the mayo by hand in a large bowl, using a stiff whisk).

If the mayo starts to split, it's not the end of the world. Pop another egg yolk into a clean bowl and then trickle in the split mixture, whisking all the time. This should bring the mayo back together and you can then finish adding the oil you have left.

If you want a slightly looser consistency, once all the oil has been incorporated, add a little water, 1 tsp at a time, until the desired consistency is reached. Season with salt and pepper to taste.

After about 30 minutes, give the mayo a stir and taste to check the seasoning. Refrigerate and use within 2 days.

Variations

Aïoli
Add 2 grated garlic cloves and an extra squeeze of lemon at the start. Serve with raw veg, such as cucumber, carrot, pepper and courgette batons, or blanched asparagus or cauliflower florets; or cold chicken, roast beef or shellfish.

Tartare sauce

This goes brilliantly with fish and chips. Finely chop ½ cucumber, 1 shallot, 1 tsp capers and the leaves from 4 sprigs of dill. Stir through the finished mayonnaise.

Lemon and chive mayo

Another great sauce to serve with fish. Add the juice of 1 lemon and 20g chives, finely chopped, to the finished mayonnaise.

Mustard mayo

This is particularly good in a sandwich with ham or beef. Add an extra 2 tsp English mustard to the mayo ingredients at the start.

Chipotle mayo

A delicious spicy dipping sauce for chips, roasted potato wedges or raw veg. Add as many dried chipotle chilli flakes (at least a generous pinch) to the finished mayo as you dare! Leave to stand for an hour and then stir to ensure the chilli heat spreads through the mayo.

Curried mayo

This is a great dipping sauce for batons of crunchy veg, or you can use it to make a spicy potato salad or serve it with cold chicken or turkey. Add 2 tsp good-quality, medium-hot curry powder and the juice of 1 lime to the finished mayo and mix thoroughly to combine. Roughly chop the leaves from a small bunch (20g) of coriander; finely chop the leaves from a couple of mint sprigs. Stir the chopped herbs through the curried mayo.

Blue cheese dip

The ideal dip for nachos and roasted potato wedges. To the finished mayo, add 100g strong crumbly blue cheese, finely crumbled, 100g natural yoghurt and an extra grinding of black pepper. Beat together to blend the blue cheese through the mayo.

French dressing

This is the Jack-of-all-trades dressing. It's become so widely used because it's so versatile and we all love it! At River Cottage we add fresh thyme leaves to give it a delightful herby note. It's the ideal go-to dressing when you want to liven up a simple assembly of crisp leaves or crunchy veg.

Makes 500ml

2 tbsp Dijon mustard
50ml cider vinegar
½ garlic clove, finely grated
4 sprigs of thyme, leaves picked
Juice of 1 lemon
300ml extra virgin olive or
  cold-pressed rapeseed oil
75ml water
Sea salt and black pepper

Put the mustard, cider vinegar, garlic, thyme leaves and lemon juice into a food processor and blitz to combine.

With the motor running, trickle in the olive or rapeseed oil through the feeder tube, followed by the water. Blend until the dressing is fully emulsified. Season with sea salt and pepper to taste.

The dressing will keep in a sealed clean jar in the fridge for up to a month. You'll need to shake it to re-emulsify before using.

Swaps
For a feistier dressing, use English rather than Dijon mustard. If you fancy a dressing with a nice aniseed hint, swap the thyme with tarragon.

Roast garlic and anchovy dressing

Roasting garlic mellows the taste, giving it a delicious sweetness and depth of flavour. It's the basis for this exceptional dressing, which will enhance almost any salad and is also amazing tossed through roasted veg, especially purple sprouting broccoli and kale. It's a great one to have to hand to take a simple salad to the next level.

Makes about 200ml

1 whole garlic bulb (50–75g)
5 tinned or jarred anchovy fillets (MSC certified)
Juice of 1 lemon
50ml sunflower oil
60ml extra virgin olive oil or cold-pressed rapeseed oil
Sea salt and black pepper

Preheat the oven to 180°C/Fan 160°C/Gas 4. Wrap the whole garlic tightly in foil and roast in the oven for 40–50 minutes, or until it feels completely soft when you squeeze it. Set aside to cool.

Once cooled, cut a thin slice off the root end of the garlic to reveal the individual cloves, which will be a deep brown colour now. Squeeze each one from the tip end and the garlic should easily slip out of the skin. Don't forget to scoop out any garlic flesh left in the slice you've taken from the root.

Put all the garlic flesh into a small food processor with the anchovies, lemon juice and both oils. Blitz thoroughly to combine and emulsify. Season the dressing with salt and pepper to taste, bearing in mind that the anchovies contribute salt so you won't need to add much, if any.

Keep the dressing in a clean jar in the fridge and use within a week. It may split in the fridge but just give it a good shake before use to re-emulsify.

Swaps
For a veggie version of this dressing, omit the anchovies and replace with 2 tbsp capers.

Lemon and garlic dressing

This is a great dressing for punchy green leaves. By including the zest of the lemon – as well as the juice – you get a truer lemon flavour and a better texture. Keep it in a jar in the fridge and don't just save it for salads. It goes particularly well on freshly cooked greens, such as kale and chard, and you can use it to dress any kind of potato.

Makes 500ml

2 lemons
3 garlic cloves, roughly chopped
150ml extra virgin olive oil
150ml cold-pressed rapeseed oil
1 tsp honey
Sea salt and black pepper

Finely grate the zest from the lemons and set it aside. Cut a thin slice from the top and bottom of the lemons, then stand on a board and slice off the skin and pith.

Put the lemon flesh and grated zest into a jug blender and add the garlic, olive and rapeseed oils and the honey. Blitz thoroughly to combine. Season with salt and pepper to taste. You want a smooth dressing so, if necessary, strain it through a fine sieve to remove any little pieces of lemon pip.

Keep the dressing in a clean jar in the fridge and use within a couple of weeks.

Swaps
For a sweeter note, use a large orange instead of the couple of lemons.

Soy, lime, chilli, ginger and garlic dressing

This beauty of a dressing is great with any crunchy veg, giving heat and depth. Jar it up, keep it in the fridge, and if you happen to be cooking some noodles or rice, toss them with a spoonful or two to pep them up. If you want a slightly less hot version, deseed the chilli first.

Makes 250ml

2 limes
2 garlic cloves, roughly chopped
50g fresh ginger, roughly chopped
1 red chilli, stem removed
200ml tamari (or soy sauce)

Finely grate the zest from the limes and set it aside. Cut a thin slice from the top and bottom of the limes, then stand on a board and slice off the skin and pith.

Put the lime flesh into a jug blender and add the garlic, ginger, chilli, lime zest and tamari. Blitz thoroughly until you have a smooth dressing. If necessary, strain through a fine sieve to remove any little pieces of lime pip.

Keep the dressing in a clean jar in the fridge and use within a couple of weeks.

Swaps
For a nuttier dressing, switch out the ginger and add 1 tbsp toasted sesame seeds instead.

Orange, kimchi and seaweed dressing

Full of rich umami flavours, this dressing is simple and quick to make but delivers a big punch. It will lift any raw veg but works particularly well with bitter leaves, such as chicory or cooked brassicas, especially roast cauliflower.

Makes 1 small jar

2 oranges
50g kimchi (or Kimkraut, see
   page 232)
20g organic mixed seaweed flakes
   or nori sheets
1 tbsp tamari (or soy sauce)
2 tbsp cold-pressed rapeseed oil

Cut a thin slice from the top and bottom of the oranges, then stand them on a board and slice off the skin and pith.

Put the orange flesh into a jug blender and add the kimchi or Kimkraut, seaweed, tamari and rapeseed oil. Blitz thoroughly, then strain through a fine sieve.

Keep the dressing in a clean jar in the fridge and use within a week.

Swaps

For a spicy version of this dressing, use a deseeded red chilli in place of the seaweed.

Quick pickles

This is a quick and hassle-free way of creating pickled veg in no time at all. In fact, these pickles can be eaten as soon as they cool down but will keep in the fridge in a sealed container for up to a month. This recipe works especially well with red onions, carrots, beetroot and cauliflower – or a combination of these. Pickled veg works brilliantly in salads, lending a bright, zingy contrast to salad leaves and other green veg.

Makes 250g

250g vegetables of your choice
  (red onions, carrots, beetroot,
  cauliflower, or a mix)
200ml cider vinegar
200ml water
1 tsp fennel seeds
1 tsp coriander seeds
1 tsp cumin seeds
A pinch of sea salt

Prepare your chosen vegetables: peel, halve and finely slice onions; peel and thinly slice carrots or pare them into ribbons with a veg peeler; peel and finely slice or dice beetroot; break cauliflower into small florets. Put the veg into a bowl.

Pour the cider vinegar and water into a saucepan and add the fennel, coriander and cumin seeds. Slowly bring to the boil over a low heat to infuse the liquid with the spice seeds, then remove from the heat and strain through a sieve into a jug to remove the seeds.

Pour the hot strained liquor over your chosen veg, making sure they are completely covered, and leave to cool.

Pack any pickled veg that you won't be using straight away into a sterilised jar (see page 232), making sure they are submerged in the pickling liquor. Seal with a tight-fitting lid, keep in the fridge and use within a month.

Kimkraut

This recipe was created in the River Cottage kitchen while trying to achieve the character of kimchi without the key ingredient – Chinese cabbage. As this vegetable's growing season is so short in this country, we used white cabbage instead. On tasting it, Hugh instantly called it kimkraut, an apt name as you really get the best of kimchi and sauerkraut: the ginger, chilli and garlic from the kimchi and that great cabbage crunch from sauerkraut. It's become one of our absolute staples and we always have a batch on the go. You'll need a 1kg jar with a non-corrosive lid, and another smaller jar to hand for any excess.

Makes a 1kg jar (at least)

750g white cabbage
1 large carrot (about 100g)
1 apple, cored
1 medium-hot red chilli, finely sliced
100g fresh ginger, grated
3 garlic cloves (about 15g), grated
30g kelp or dulse flakes (or
    4 tbsp fish sauce if you can't
    find seaweed)
50g sweet paprika
Fine sea salt

First you need to sterilise the jar. Preheat the oven to 130°C/Fan 110°C/Gas 1. Thoroughly clean your jar and lid – even if it's new, give it a good wash. Place the jar in the oven for 10 minutes, then pop the lid in and leave for another minute. Take the jar and lid from the oven, being careful not to touch the insides. Leave to cool completely.

Remove a few outer leaves from the cabbage and set aside for later. Cut away the fibrous base of the stem then finely shred the cabbage and place in a large bowl.

Grate the carrot and apple and add to the shredded cabbage with the chilli, ginger, garlic, seaweed or fish sauce and paprika. Toss to mix.

Now weigh the combined veg mix to calculate how much salt to add: you need 2% salt. So, for example, if there is 1kg veg you need 20g fine sea salt. Add the salt to the veg and firmly massage it in with your hands until the veg begins to soften.

Pack the veg into the sterilised jar, leaving at least 4cm space at the top of the jar. Don't be tempted to overfill it – you can always use another smaller jar!

Now make a quick brine, ratio 2% salt to water: dissolve 10g salt in 500ml water. Pour enough brine into the jar to cover the veg and then keep the rest of the brine in a sealed container in case you need it later. Secure the lid and turn the jar upside down. Repeat this a few times to get the brine to fill any air gaps.

Remove the lid and then place the reserved cabbage leaves on top of the veg mix. Push them down, being careful not to spurt out the brine. Once you can push down no further you need to weigh the top down to keep all the veg submerged under the brine. The weight must be non-corrosive: I use a small ceramic ramekin; Hugh uses thoroughly cleaned pebbles from the beach!

Secure the lid tightly and place the jar on a tray to catch any juices. Leave at room temperature, not a spot where the temperature varies significantly, for 24 hours.

The next day, slowly loosen the lid (this is called burping). You should have a good fizz and some liquid will leak out of the top. If too much liquid escapes and the veg become exposed to air, top up with some of the brine. Secure the lid again and repeat this process every day.

Allow the veg to ferment for 5–14 days, depending on the ambient temperature and how you like it to taste: the less fermentation time the crunchier the veg will be; the longer the ferment the softer and more intense the flavour. After experimenting a few times you'll find your sweet spot.

Once you reach your ideal flavour, make sure there is enough liquid to cover the veg; if not top up with some reserved brine. Secure the lid and refrigerate to arrest the fermentation. As long as the veg is covered in brine the kraut will keep for months.

Swaps
Use smoke-dried chipotle chilli flakes instead of the fresh chilli and swap out half of the sweet paprika for smoked paprika to give the kraut a deep, smoky flavour.

Red cabbage, beetroot, juniper and bay kraut

Fermenting veg can seem intimidating but it's relatively straightforward and this no-fuss recipe will give you a kraut with bags of flavour and colour. Just watch out for the juniper berries when you're eating it as they are super powerful. Oh, and be warned, it's really purple and will stain almost anything! Have another small jar sterilised and ready in case you have more than will fit into the big jar.

Makes a 1kg jar (at least)

About 750g red cabbage
About 150g beetroot
15 juniper berries, lightly bashed
10 bay leaves
Fine sea salt and black pepper

First you need to sterilise the jar. Preheat the oven to 130°C/Fan 110°C/Gas 1. Thoroughly clean your jar and lid – even if it's new, give it a good wash. Place the jar in the oven for 10 minutes, then pop the lid in and leave for another minute. Take the jar and lid from the oven, being careful not to touch the insides. Leave to cool completely.

Remove a few outer leaves from the cabbage and set aside for later. Cut away the fibrous base of the stem then finely shred the cabbage and place in a large bowl. Peel and grate the beetroot and add to the shredded cabbage with the juniper berries and bay leaves. Toss to mix.

Now weigh the combined veg mix to calculate how much salt to add: you need 2% salt. So, for example, if there is 1kg veg you need 20g fine sea salt. Add the salt to the veg and firmly massage it in with your hands until the veg begins to soften and release some liquid.

Pack the veg into the sterilised jar, leaving at least 4cm space at the top of the jar. Don't be tempted to overfill it – you can always use another smaller jar!

If the veg doesn't release enough moisture to cover it in the jar you'll need to make a quick brine (2% salt to water) to top it up. Simply dissolve 10g salt in 500ml water. Pour enough brine into the jar to cover the veg and then keep the rest of the brine in a sealed container in case you need it later. Secure the lid and turn the jar upside down. Repeat this a few times to get the brine to fill any air gaps.

Remove the lid and then place the reserved cabbage leaves on top of the veg mix. Push them down, being careful not to spurt out the brine. Once you can push down no further you need to weigh the top down to keep all the veg submerged under the brine. The weight must be non-corrosive: I use a small ceramic ramekin.

Secure the lid tightly and place the jar on a tray to catch any juices. Leave at room temperature, not a spot where the temperature varies significantly, for 24 hours.

The next day, slowly loosen the lid (this is called burping). You should have a good fizz and some liquid will leak out of the top. If too much liquid escapes and the veg become exposed to air, top up with some of the brine. Secure the lid again and repeat this process every day.

Allow the veg to ferment for 5–14 days, depending on the ambient temperature and how you like it to taste: the less fermentation time the crunchier the veg will be; the longer the ferment the softer and more intense the flavour. After experimenting a few times you'll find your sweet spot.

Once you reach your ideal flavour, make sure there is enough liquid to cover the veg; if not top up with some reserved brine. Secure the lid and refrigerate to arrest the fermentation. As long as the veg is covered in brine the kraut will keep for months.

Swaps
For a festive version, replace the bay and juniper with a few star anise, a cinnamon stick and a couple of cloves.

Directory

We have such amazing farmers, growers and producers in the UK that we should all do our best to support them. Buying SLOW – seasonal, local, organic and wild – is one of our core values at River Cottage, so we'd love to share with you some of our favourite suppliers. Some of these are local to the farm, but I've included great options that are available nationwide, too.

Veg

Our neighbours, Ash and Kate, at the truly brilliant Trill Farm supply organic veg boxes, delivering around the Axminster and Lyme Regis areas.
www.trillfarmgarden.co.uk

Riverford Organic Farmers have been trailblazers for organic growing since 1986. They deliver organic veg boxes to your door nationwide.
www.riverford.co.uk

Abel & Cole offer a great selection of organic fruit and vegetables delivered to your door, as well as many more wonderful organic essentials.
www.abelandcole.co.uk

Meat

Harry and Emily run a fantastic regenerative, organic farm just 2 miles as the crow flies from River Cottage. Haye Farm supplies organic meat and lots of other organic goodies, with deliveries nationwide.
www.hayefarmdevon.co.uk

Coombe Farm Organic offers a range of superb organic meats, specialising in retired dairy beef, which is well worth a try.
www.coombefarmorganic.co.uk

Fish

Based at our local farm shop (Millers), Lyme Bay Fish Shack, run by Nigel and Corinne, offers a great array of fish caught with rod and line or static net from their own boat, as well as other boats landing in Lyme Regis. Collection only.
www.millersfarmshop.co.uk

Pesky Fish is an amazing online fishmonger, with a keen eye on sustainability, connecting the fishermen directly with the consumer. They have a daily market to buy from and the fish is delivered to your door in recyclable packaging.
www.peskyfish.co.uk

Oils

Shipped by Sail import some amazing olive oil from Portugal and its all shipped here under sail power! You can't get olive oil with a better flavour – and story – anywhere.
www.shippedbysail.org

Organic Yorkshire rapeseed oil, produced by Mike Stringer, is a real treat. You can get it from Hodmedods while shopping for your pulses.
www.hodmedods.co.uk

Pulses and grains

Hodmedods supply all our pulses and grains – everything from lentils to quinoa – all farmed in the UK and delivered nationwide.
www.hodmedods.co.uk

Dairy

Riverford Organics supply outstanding dairy products as well as vegetables.
www.riverford.co.uk

Milk & More supply dairy products including milk in glass bottles delivered to your door just like milkmen did! They also stock lots of other essentials. Try to pick from their organic range.
www.milkandmore.co.uk

General organic suppliers

Planet Organic is a great one-stop organic shop for all your staples.
www.planetorganic.com

Whole Foods Online is another excellent organic supplier, perfect for topping up your storecupboard.
www.buywholefoodsonline.co.uk

Index

Acknowledgements

Any book is always a team effort and I have been lucky enough to work with a fantastic bunch of talented folk who have made this book come to life in so many ways. I'm incredibly grateful to them all.

First though, Hayley and Willow, my crazy family, thank you for putting up with the late nights, missed dinners and the grumpiness. Without you, simply none of this would have been possible. You're everything to me.

To Hugh Fearnley-Whittingstall, for inspiring not only me but a whole generation of cooks to think differently. It's been a true pleasure to work so closely with you over the last ten years; long may it continue.

I'm grateful to Rachel de Thample for making this book read like a dream. Rachel is a true talent in her own right and it's been a great pleasure to collaborate on this book.

Thanks to Gill Meller, whom I've known as long as anyone at River Cottage, for lending me his artistic genius. It's always been a joy and a privilege to cook alongside you, Gill.

Photographer Emma Lee and her assistants managed to capture the essence of River Cottage with a calm and ease which was astounding. Thanks to you for making this book the visual masterpiece it is. I can't wait for our next adventure!

To Rowan Yapp, Kitty Stogdon and the rest of the team at Bloomsbury, thank you for your patience and gentle but firm encouragement to stay on track. Janet Illsley and Will Webb, you have brought this book together as only you can. I can't wait to work with you all again.

Bob, without whom I think River Cottage would cease to exist, you've been a great friend, colleague and support, for which you have my eternal thanks.

To all the members of the River Cottage team, both past and present, who have inspired me in one way or another. Special thanks to Steven Kiernan, Adam Crofts, Andy Tyrell, Joel Gosling, Rosanna Unwin, Ashley Darling, Chrissy Styles, Connor Reid, Mark McCabe, Sam Lomas, Jack Botha, Josh Bond, Daniel Harding and many, many more. You're all legends in my eyes.

To Stewart Dodd, for being the best boss and a better friend, thanks for this opportunity and for putting up with me. I know I'm not easy, but I've always appreciated your unwavering support more than I can ever convey to you.

And finally, to Mum, Dad, Jesse, Joni and Amelle, for all our time together. I'm grateful for every minute and there is a little bit of each of you in this book. I love you all and I promise to grow up one day.

River Cottage: Food to Inspire Change

From the moment River Cottage came to our TV screens, Hugh has championed a more holistic and sustainable approach to food. He wants us to know where our food comes from, and to understand the consequences of our food choices. For almost three decades now, River Cottage and Hugh have been showing us that food can inspire change – both in our lives and in the world around us.

Hugh Fearnley-Whittingstall and his partners at Keo Films created the original River Cottage television series in 1999. The shows ran on Channel 4 in the UK for the next 15 years. The series charted Hugh's culinary adventures, first as a downsizing smallholder at the original River Cottage in West Dorset, and later as he established his cookery school and events venue at the more expansive Park Farm.

River Cottage HQ is now a 90-acre property in an Area of Outstanding Natural Beauty on the Devon/Dorset border. The site was developed and designed under the guidance of architect and sustainability specialist Stewart Dodd, now Chief Executive at River Cottage. Gelf Alderson has been Hugh's chief collaborator since 2012. Hugh, Gelf and their team of chef-tutors now welcome guests from all over the world, teaching them not only how to improve their cooking techniques and artisan food skills, but also how to grow their own ingredients and source food in an ethical and sustainable way.

River Cottage HQ has won many awards, including 'Best Cookery School' in the Great British Food Awards, for the past 4 years running. The River Cottage Online Cooking Diploma was launched in 2020 and the Next Level Diploma the following year.

Guests can also stay at Park Farm's beautifully restored seventeenth-century farmhouse and feast on seasonal, local, organic and wild food at regular events in the threshing barn. The River Cottage Kitchen and Store, a restaurant sourcing ingredients from Park Farm and neighbouring organic growers, opened on the site in the spring of 2022.

Hugh and River Cottage have published more than 30 books, including the popular River Cottage Handbook series of practical manuals on artisan cooking techniques, gardening, smallholding and foraging. These books have sold over 2 million copies and won multiple awards, including the Glenfiddich Award, Guild of Food Writers Award, the André Simon Award and, in the US, the James Beard Award.

River Cottage also produces a range of ethically sourced organic products, including yoghurt, kombucha, kefir, sauerkrauts, stocks, sauces, wines, beers and ciders.

BLOOMSBURY PUBLISHING
Bloomsbury Publishing Plc
50 Bedford Square, London, WC1B 3DP, UK
29 Earlsfort Terrace, Dublin 2, Ireland

BLOOMSBURY, BLOOMSBURY PUBLISHING and the Diana logo are trademarks
of Bloomsbury Publishing Plc

First published in Great Britain 2022

A catalogue record for this book is available from the British Library

ISBN: HB: 978-1-5266-3910-3; eBook: 978-1-5266-3911-0

10 9 8 7 6 5 4 3 2 1

Project Editor: Janet Illsley
Designer: Will Webb
Photographer: Emma Lee
Illustrator: Greg Heinimann
Food Stylists: Gelf Alderson and Gill Meller
Indexer: Hilary Bird

Printed and bound in Italy by Graphicom

To find out more about our authors and books visit www.bloomsbury.com and sign
up for our newsletters